BEYOND the STYLE MANUAL

BUNDLE #1

RED ADEPT PUBLISHING

HOOK, TAGLINE, and SINKER

GET TO the POINT

HE SAID, SHE SAID

RED ADEPT
PUBLISHING
Unlocking New Worlds

Style Guide Bundle #1
A Red Adept Publishing Book
Copyright © 2015. All rights reserved.
First Print Edition: October 2015

Red Adept Publishing, LLC
104 Bugenfield Court
Garner, NC 27529
http://RedAdeptPublishing.com/
Cover and Formatting: Streetlight Graphics

TABLE OF CONTENTS

BEYOND the STYLE MANUAL

RED ADEPT PUBLISHING

HOOK, TAGLINE, and SINKER

WRITING IRRESISTIBLE BOOK DESCRIPTIONS

INTRODUCTION

WHAT'S A BOOK DESCRIPTION, AND WHY DO I NEED TO SPEND SO MUCH TIME ON IT? WHY DO I NEED THIS GUIDE?

A book description is an enticing summary of the main character(s), setting, and conflict in your fiction book. It's the back cover copy, the lines of text everyone reads to see if they like the book enough to buy it.

It's also an example of your writing skills. A single awkward phrase, typo, or missed comma can persuade a significant number of your potential readers to look elsewhere. How can they trust that someone who can't manage a few paragraphs can pen a well-crafted novel? Readers often suspect this of indie authors due to the perception that many indie books are badly written, poorly edited, or both. A shiny book description can ease any subconscious concern that your potential readers have about the quality of your writing.

Browsing readers generally look at the cover art first, and if they're pleased with that, they look at your book description. You need both to be in tiptop shape to make a sale.

Tiptop shape, for a book description, means promising something your target audience thinks they can't live without. Get it a little wrong, and your sales will fall short of their potential. Get it very wrong, and your book will get angry one-star reviews complaining about being misled.

Save your book from obscurity by writing an irresistible description.

WHY IS IT SO HARD TO WRITE A FEW PARAGRAPHS WHEN I JUST POUNDED OUT TENS OF THOUSANDS OF WORDS FOR MY NOVEL?

It's hard precisely because you know each and every one of those tens of thousands of words. How do you choose? Which are the best? How do you decide which characters and plot points to mention? Authors always have the hardest time writing their own book descriptions because so many minor details contribute to the collective awesomeness of the story and they love them all. After all, they chose those parts for their books.

Writing an awesome book description can take weeks. Or it can take half an hour. It all depends on how familiar you are with the aspects of a great book description and how well you apply it to your specific book.

WHAT'S THE DIFFERENCE BETWEEN A BOOK DESCRIPTION AND A BLURB? ARE THERE OTHER TERMS THAT I MIGHT BE GETTING CONFUSED WITH EACH OTHER?

A book description is generally no more than two hundred words contained in no more than four paragraphs that describe the basic premise of the book without giving spoilers. Its entire purpose is to entice the reader to purchase the book in order to learn the rest of the story.

A blurb is praise for your book from another author, one whose name will be recognized by your readers. Another term for this is a *testimonial*. They generally look like this:

"Couldn't put it down... had me up until 4:00 a.m.!"

—*Rich McFamous, author of That Book*

"A wild and rollicking ride that will have your head spinning and your sides splitting!"

—*Regina Puzzlova, bestselling author of Dying to Read It*

In addition, a book description is not a *synopsis*. A synopsis is a summary of the whole story, including the very end. It's usually defined by word count or length, such as one thousand words or one page, and is submitted to agents or publishing houses, depending on their specific guidelines. Professionals in the publishing industry need to know the end of your book. Potential readers don't. So in your book descriptions: *no spoilers*.

A *sentence summary* is twenty-five words or less, a one-line summary that's handy to memorize in case anyone asks you out of the blue what your book is about. It's really difficult to sum up sixty, eighty, or one hundred thousand words in one sentence unless you've prepared ahead of time. Having a sentence summary ready makes you look more like you know what you're doing with this whole writing-books thing.

BASICS: GATHERING YOUR INGREDIENTS

C REATING A BOOK DESCRIPTION IS a lot like writing a book. You need all the proper ingredients close at hand before you begin. The ingredients for a book description vary from book to book, and you may not use each of them every time, but if you leave out a critical ingredient, the result is going to taste a little funny to your readers.

Have the following story elements gathered when you create your book description:

THE NAME OF YOUR PROTAGONIST

Whether you give your character's first name, full name, or nickname, or you introduce them as the stranger known only by a catchy bandit or mafioso name, you'll need to identify the character by some specific appellation for the benefit of your readers early on in the description, preferably in the first sentence.

PROTAGONIST'S JOB AND AGE (RANGE)

Book descriptions often classify the main character in the first sentence with a reference to age and/or job. Compacting this basic information into the first part of the description gives the reader a specific group of categories to place the character into before getting distracted with all the excitement of the rest of the description. This condensed information helps them determine whether they will relate strongly to the character and, by extension, whether they will enjoy your book.

"Tom Dickinson had been a long-haul trucker for over thirty years, but one night's fateful decision..."

"Sixteen-year-old Maisie Smith has never kissed a boy, but when..."

"When detective Susan Wilkins gets the call that yet another copycat..."

PROTAGONIST'S STATUS QUO AND/OR AN EARLY TRIGGER EVENT THAT DRAGS THEM INTO THE PLOT

Many first sentences give the main character's status quo: what we find them doing when the book opens. Often, characters have their own expectations for their immediate futures, which have nothing to do with the plot about to ambush them. If you are planning a sudden reversal of fortune for your heroes, including what they expect as well as what actually happens to them is good fodder for hooking readers. Another option is to skip mentioning the status quo if it is not attached to important setting or plot details; choose instead to begin the first sentence with the trigger event that draws the character, sometimes reluctantly, into the main body of the plot.

"All that West Texas rancher Dawson Mills wanted to get done that morning was to move his cattle to the north hills. But an angel in a bedazzled Stetson had other plans for him."

"Alistair's evening soirée plans veer sharply into the surreal when his redheaded escort jams a pistol into his ribs and tells him to drive to the Czech Republic."

PROTAGONIST'S GOALS

Everyone wakes up in the morning with a plan to get something specific done that day. We may never realize our goals—*maybe tomorrow, laundry*—but we have them nonetheless. Characters can have all kinds of goals at the beginning of the story. Some may get accomplished, and others may be abandoned or remain forever unresolved. Characters may have goals that have nothing to do with the plot that's about to take over their lives, or they may be the sort of characters who pursue their goals single-mindedly and wrestle their success into existence at the end of the book.

No matter what happens to your characters and their goals, they woke up that first morning with something they wanted to get done. Sharing what's important to your characters lets readers empathize with them.

> "Second-year law student Peach McCoy chalks her top marks up to her slow-burning dedication to personally put away her father's murderer."

> "Saul Eberhardt wanted to go to space ever since he caught that first faint flash of *Sputnik* in the night sky over his parents' Montana farm."

PROTAGONIST'S MOTIVE(S) FOR PURSUING THOSE GOALS

Everybody wants something, but *why* they want it is a whole other story, and hinting at your characters' motives can be an excellent way to show their personalities. Is the hot doctor helping your main character because he's in love with her, or is he helping her because he has his own nefarious plans for her? Dun dun *dunnn*! Chances are you don't want to say too much, in case it gives away important plot points, but you can always ask the question and leave both options open for your reader to guess at.

> "When Doctor Foxy McSwoon looks into her eyes, Betty can't help the heat that rises within her. But does he merely want to tear her clothes off, or do his desires run claw deep?"

EARLY CONFLICT, DIFFICULTIES, AND OBSTACLES

It's no fun if everybody just dances their way to the end of the book without any trouble at all. Conflict is what builds character, quite literally, throughout the course of a book. So when you're writing your book description, keep in mind the first difficulties that your protagonist comes up against. Do his allies not want to work with him? Is her best friend already dating the guy who can't keep his eyes off her? Has the most obvious suspect also been found murdered?

"The High Council, however, is in Lord Grievard's pocket and has plenty of shiny, golden reasons not to listen to Armessa's calls to action."

"Detective Statlett would arrest the bastard for kidnapping and torture, except she accidentally offered his mangled corpse a quarter to play *Just Died in Your Arms*."

PROTAGONIST'S FLAWS

Character flaws make the heroic people we read about seem more human, more relatable, and they give us hope that someday, we, too, might be heroic. We love it when they don't know what to say, when they can't immediately think of the next step, when they miss something obvious, and when they beat themselves up for it. We do those things all the time. We love it when they bear scars, have anger issues, or can't stop thinking about that one thing so long ago that was never resolved. We do those things all the time, too. Flaws can be conveyed in a book description with just a few words, and they can be tied in with other strong word choices that match the same emotional tone as the flaw.

"Passion rules painter Berenice Anderton's life: it fills her art with impossible beauty and detail, and it hooks her up with questionable substances and strangers in bar bathroom stalls."

"Niccola can't live without Katye, so after her adopted sister dies in a tragic car accident, Niccola throws away her new promotion and follows her sister to the spirit world."

WHO OR WHAT YOUR MAIN ANTAGONIST IS

Most books contain an external antagonist, a physical being outside the mind of the protagonist whose goals are contradictory to the hero's. But nemeses can come in many forms. These include, but are definitely not limited, to internal psychological issues; computer constructs; poor timing; gods; a series of unfortunate, unrelated events; and fate. Whatever your protagonist is up against, it's going to need some kind of mention in the book description.

Hook, Tagline, and Sinker

> "Yancy never expected his Arachne tattoo to bridge time, space, and myth. He certainly never expected the bitter loser in a weaving contest with the goddess Athena to begin manifesting in his bedroom at night, demanding that he carry out the schemes she wove, either."

ANTAGONIST'S GOALS, MOTIVES, AND FLAWS

Depending on your book, these may not be necessary. But if your antagonist is nearly as large a part of the book as your protagonist, then strongly consider giving him his own paragraph.

> "But Loric could never resist that dark call within, not like Danner did. He finds strength in his own darkness, something Danner won't let himself possess. His cop brother might figure out Loric's the Barbie Doll Butcher, but all that's going to earn him is the next slot on Loric's kill list."

THE FINAL CONFLICT

Your final conflict should never explicitly make it into your book description, but you need to make sure you are aware of the events that take place as well as their significance to your plot. Is it a clash of cheerleader wills, an actual battle, a struggle to overcome the protagonist's fear in order to save someone she loves, or maybe confronting a serial killer? Will there be love, sacrifice, or rare hybrid puppies? Does everybody die? Whatever giant clash you have planned for the end of your book, you'll need to allude—and *only* allude—to it in some enticing way at the end of your blurb.

> "If she can't find a way out, Maura might have to choose between the man who gave her that first big break and the soulful spirit whose voice made her a star."

> "When sudden tragedy ignites inside Gemini airspace, Admiral Styx could lose a lifetime of achievement—and the one person who believes his tale—defending his planet against his oldest enemy."

WHAT FAILURE WOULD MEAN FOR THE PROTAGONIST

All conflict carries consequence. If your good guys win, your bad guys probably lose in some way that carries negative consequences for them. Naturally, readers are more interested in what's at stake for the good guys. What should readers be afraid might happen if the good guys fail, whether partially or completely?

A handy tool in your description-writing toolbox can be to describe what's at stake through the point of view of your main character. Maybe that character has the whole picture, but maybe he doesn't. The character may believe right up until the end, like a certain young boy wizard, that he has to die in order to save others. The book will take the reader in a different direction at the proper moment, but generally, readers will take the blurb at face value and believe what the character believes. Subtle misdirection is a beautiful thing.

"One of them is going to die."

"The fate of the tri-galactic wormnet lies in Glitch Patten's hands, and war is his only option. But if he bankrupts Shaia's saga in the process, she'll delete him."

TWEAKING THE RECIPE

NOW THAT YOU HAVE GATHERED all your basic ingredients for your book description, it's time to begin thinking about what flavors you want readers to taste when they take a bite.

At its most basic, a book description simply says, "This story is about character X as he tries to do Y in the face of problem Z." These three things are your flour, sugar, and eggs—your basics. Everything else you include is spice. But which spices should you choose?

There are dozens of ways to describe the same book. You want to pick one that gives readers a hint of the big picture within your story, something meaty they can look forward to devouring. You want to show them that your book is not a cliché but that it does fall firmly within its genre borders.

Consider the following questions when you think about which angles may work best to tell your target audience about your story.

WHAT IS MY BOOK'S BIG QUESTION?

This can be as basic a question as:

"Will John save Elizabeth from the pirates?" or "Will the sheriff have a change of heart and let his brother the bandit escape at the end?"

Or, depending on your plot and tone, the question could be more philosophical than plot related, such as:

"Is it possible for AI to truly experience humanity?"

"Does true love conquer all?"

"Is it possible to start over?"

WHAT'S THE ONE THING I WANT MY READERS TO REMEMBER ABOUT MY BOOK?

Maybe you have a main character who's larger than life, or maybe your plot is punctuated by poignant moments of wisdom. Maybe the twist at the end is absolutely epic. Maybe your main character makes an early, offhand choice that affects the rest of the plot, and he comes to regret it more and more strongly. Find the emotional nugget that captures the feeling you want people to take away with them, the one thing you want them to mention to their friends when they talk about your book. Then promise it to them in your description.

> "But nothing could prepare Lisette for the horrific realization that she herself had been the instrument of Luc's death."

> "When Fillip fills his elective slot for the fall semester with a random finger-point into the class listings, he unwittingly seals his fate with his own hand."

WHAT'S SPECIAL ABOUT MY PLOT DEVICE? WHY IS MY BOOK DIFFERENT FROM ANY OTHERS?

Do you have a fresh take on a classic theme? Are you retelling or doing a gritty reboot of an old myth or fable? Does your love triangle have an unexpected corner? Do you have unique parallels between various elements of your plot or characters that you've never seen anywhere else? Is your setting absolutely mind blowing? Are you taking on a period in history that few authors have dared to touch? Does your story address a fresh, emerging theme that's breaking into the public consciousness?

> "Harold Marken never reconciled with his son's homosexuality until after Tom's death. But suspicious circumstances, and Harold's deep love for the towheaded boy who used to ride on his shoulders at the lake every summer, drive him to look deeper into Tom's supposed suicide—and into his own heart."

"Prince Charming needs someone's heart, and from what he's heard, Hansel and Gretel are just the assassins he needs to get the job done. After all, Snow White's already come back from the dead once."

IF YOUR BOOK FITS IN ONLY ONE GENRE, HOW DOES IT REPRESENT THAT GENRE, AND WHAT MAKES IT STAND OUT?

Every genre has tropes, as anyone who's ever gotten sucked in over on tvtropes.org can attest. What makes a book fresh and original is its approach to tropes. Mixing and matching familiar concepts with new ideas and details presents the readers with something fresh.

Or perhaps what makes your book stand out is its mix of two, three, or even four genres. Does it have one central genre, surrounded by a supporting cast? Is it relatively equal across the board? Do you have a new take on any one of your genres?

"No princess, especially one as rebellious as Briannica, wants to be married off to a loser prince. But when the knife-throwing competition among her three suitors goes horribly awry, she's forced to flee with the circus members who managed not to get arrested by her apoplectic father."

"All James wanted after he inherited his uncle's estate was solitude and solace. The divorce strained his health, and his high-pressure job killed his soul. His attractive yet quirky neighbor, Jules, offers other options, though, and soon, James is gamely stargazing with her at midnight. But a new light in the sky promises a dimensional shift in his perception of reality, all theoretical strings attached."

A SAMPLE BITE

ABOOK DESCRIPTION SHOULD MATCH ITS book. When the description reflects its novel, it tells readers what they can expect within. It should be vibrant without being misleading, promising an exciting genre read. Readers love their tropes; they love to know they stand on familiar territory. Give them easily recognizable hints, and they will squirm at the edge of their seats.

MATCH GENRE

A good, strong genre tone helps anchor your book within its genre as well as deliver a few specific messages about its individuality within the genre. Tone is shown more through word choice than anything else. Descriptive phrases, noun and adjective choices, and the like will plant tiny seeds of expectation within your readers' minds, assuring them of more of the same inside your book. A technothriller narrated by a cynical character will have a wildly different tone than a bodice ripper narrated by a French ghost from the 1700s, and the last thing you want is for readers to expect one and get the other.

MATCH TONE

You've written a solid genre novel. Readers who love your genre will eat it up. Or will they? Some readers prefer a light, even comedic tone. Others love to revel in the dark and gritty. Perhaps your book is whimsically romantic. How do you draw the right reader? Make your description's tone match your novel's tone. The last thing you want to do is to draw in the wrong readers, even within your genre. No one likes to be misled: that path is littered with one-star reviews.

MATCH WRITING STYLE

A book description should also be an example of your writing style. If your book is lusciously lyrical, your description has to pop with exquisite turns of phrase. If you've written a rollicking comedic chick-lit caper, your description should be full of quirky references and fast-paced sentence structure. The length and pacing of your sentences should match the overall style of your book.

BOOK OR SERIES TITLE TIE-INS: USE WITH CAUTION

Does your book or series title offer a word or phrase you could tie into your book description? Consider your genre first and your book's writing style second. If your book targets a younger audience, has a comedic tone, or allows for cuteness and wordplay in some other way, such cleverness will elicit a more positive result from potential readers. Genres and plots that attract a readership that's more serious in nature will be less forgiving of descriptions that use precious word space for witticisms.

THE RULES

THESE RULES ARE REALLY MORE like guidelines, and every one of them has been broken somewhere, by some book that sold very well. Those books essentially succeeded *despite* their descriptions, an achievement that often requires mountains of work on the author's part. Readers expect certain things from book descriptions, even if they're just subconscious expectations—and those extend past titillating word choice to concepts like length and verb tense. Essentially, if you follow all of these recommendations, you'll avoid common mistakes that are far more likely to doom a book than they are to send it up the charts.

GIVE ONLY INTRODUCTIONS

Be aware of when important plot developments and character revelations take place within your book. A good book description shouldn't give away specific details past Act I, or approximately one quarter to one third of the way through the book. It doesn't matter how earth-shattering your later plot twists are—you should be able to sell your book on its premise and early development alone. Let the readers be shocked and amazed at all the other astonishing events awaiting them as your plot develops. If you honestly can't think of a single interesting thing to say about the first third of your book, you should consider rewriting it.

USE THE PROPER POV AND VERB TENSE

The industry standard for book description POV and verb tense is third person, present tense. Some of you may already have an example floating at the edge of your mind that used first-person POV or filled its exposition with past-tense verbs yet managed to make the book sound enticing. Messing with this tried-and-true formula is always a risk, though. Readers may be titillated by the unusual, but they can easily be put off by it. You're always safer sticking with what your readers will recognize as a standard layout.

DON'T USE TOO MANY PARAGRAPHS

The number of paragraphs you need in your description varies, depending on how much you need to tell your readers in order to give them the gist of your story. Some subgenres have rather exacting paragraph patterns, and we'll get to that later.

If your plot and characters are very straightforward and your story takes place on planet Earth with no additional paranormal or magical effects to hint at, you really only need one paragraph to tell your readers what's going to happen. This is especially true with sequels, when loyal readers can fill in backstory and detail for themselves.

If you have to sketch out alternate planets, governments, cultures, timelines, some magic, or other worldbuilding in order to help your readers understand the crux of your plot, or if you have multiple main or major characters, you can use up to four paragraphs in your description. If you have more than four, you risk giving away too much information or boring the reader with too much filler. In short, if the whole back cover is text or if online readers have to click the Show More link, you wrote too much.

Most books, across most genres, have two or three paragraphs of description. Remember, you only need to explain the basics. Save most of the interesting things about your book for the book itself, because even mentioning them briefly in the description could make it too long. One of the best ways to cut down on description content is to avoid mention of all subplots. Just stick to describing the main plot in your story, and then all the subplots will be happy surprises for your readers.

Don't try to cram a dozen sentences into each of your paragraphs simply to meet the recommended paragraph number, either. (See again: that Show More link.) Online reading has a much lower patience threshold, and if readers encounter a wall of text that forces them to squint, scroll, and squint a little more, not only are they going to get frustrated, but they're going to assume your entire book is made of similar walls of text. Most likely, that will be a lost sale for you.

STICK TO THE WORD COUNT

The word count in your book description depends somewhat on how complex your information is, but you should attempt to never exceed two hundred words. Simple, straightforward plots of one medium or two small paragraphs can describe a book in a hundred words or so. Complex plots or worldbuilding explanation can overstuff a description, so take care that you don't describe the details so often that they overshadow the main thrust of your story. Details are spice, not flour.

If your book only has one POV, you can generally write a shorter description because you can avoid writing paragraphs from other major characters' POVs. If you have two major characters—such as in a general romance (see the Romance genre section in Genre Specifics)—you may end up with two paragraphs, with one about each of those characters.

Many three-paragraph descriptions use the first two to discuss plot and characters then employ the third paragraph for only the final hook statement or question. If a book fits equally well into several genres, such as a YA historical paranormal romance, then you may need four paragraphs to convey the multigenre feel.

Remember that your first draft will be far from your last, so don't worry about writing far too many words when you start. You'll need to play with it in editing in order to determine which details you really want to mention and which you can cut. The general rule is: write long, edit shorter.

THE SHAPE ON THE PAGE

NOW THAT YOU HAVE EVERYTHING you need to write your book description crammed into your brain, let's start to free it onto the page. Remember, just like the process of hammering out a book, crafting a description involves writing it long then editing it shorter.

DO YOU NEED A TAGLINE?

No. Taglines are entirely optional across all genres. If the style and plot of your book lend themselves to a short, punchy phrase, a single sentence, or series of very short sentences, then by all means, use that for your tagline. If you can't condense your story into a catchy phrase of seven words or less, you're better off skipping the tagline.

Taglines generally appear on your book cover in small print, often right above or below your title. But a tagline is also an excellent way to catch a reader's eye on online market webpages and even promotional materials, such as bookmarks or flyers.

If you want to use a tagline for your story, it should appear at the top of your book description section, above the description itself, as a standalone first line. It's different than shoutlines, which are similarly short, catchy phrases that appear in all the gaps between the paragraphs of the description.

In all cases, your taglines and shoutlines need to avoid sounding cliché or meaningless. It's better to use no taglines or shoutlines than to use ones that will make your book look boring or poorly written. Phrases like "A Second Chance at Love" or "No One Gets Out Alive" are general enough that they could apply to half the genre, and they don't convey enough specific detail to catch readers' interest.

THE FIRST LINE

The first line of your description, whether you use a tagline or you delve straight into the story, is your best chance to hook your readers. The more information you can cram into it without making it a five-line, compound-complex monster, the more information your readers will have at their disposal in order to determine right away whether the book will be to their taste. That's why it's so vital to mention your character by name: for a personal connection. Also vital are the first few words you use to describe that character. Try to reference age, job, social status, and personality. Any one of these, defined in as little as one word, will set up reader expectations right off the bat. You can expound on that as the book description rolls out.

You have a few standard options for what to say in the first line. Many stories will mention the status quo that the main character is experiencing as the book opens. If the status quo is calm and peaceful or if the character is engaging in something he or she expects to continue for the foreseeable future—a relaxing vacation or a new job—the next line usually explains how things go pear shaped.

If the status quo opens with a trigger event, such as a murder, a breakup, a scientific discovery, the rest of the blurb will generally expound upon that. This can often indicate a fast-paced book, a complex plot, or both.

CONFLICT—A FIRST-PARAGRAPH NECESSITY

No matter how many characters you have, how much worldbuilding you need to explain, or how complicated the main character's status quo is, you need to mention some kind of conflict in the very first paragraph. Readers love both kinds of conflict: internal and external. Some books have more internal conflict; some have more external conflict. Some have plenty of both. But conflict is what drives the plot and character development. It's what brings all the readers to the yard. You'll want to mention it as soon as you can possibly work it in, no later than the second sentence.

A NOTE ON SENTENCES

Sometimes, you want short, punchy sentences in your book description. They serve a very specific purpose: to hand over tiny yet powerful bits of information in dramatic fashion, which should speak to the sort of book they're describing.

But considering how much information we are trying to cram into these descriptions, we often end up with compound-complex sentence structures somewhere. That's just fine, as long as you can handle the grammar and punctuation that accompany them. There's a critical difference between a sentence that properly conveys several clusters of information with clarity and order and one that simply rambles. If your sentence contains too much information, you can always break it down into more sentences.

Here's an example of a long and rambling sentence: When John wakes up that morning, he doesn't expect to see an alien at the foot of his bed, but when Navol explains that John's pancreas is the key to opening a portal to an alternate dimension that holds an ancient, long-lost device that could save Navol's homeworld from the vicious and unrelenting attacks of the so-called evolved race known as the Phek, John reluctantly agrees to a quick laparoscopic procedure for the sake of the universe, despite the fact that he has a family history of malignant hypothermia.

And here's the same information, using various sentence lengths (the compound-complex sentence is in italics): Despite his love of science fiction movies, the last thing John expects to encounter is a chubby-tentacled alien at the foot of his bed one morning. *When Navol explains that the fate of his homeworld depends on a quick laparoscopic procedure to remove John's pancreas, which will open a transdimensional portal and allow Navol to retrieve a critical piece of technology, John has more than one serious reservation.* With his medical history, the wrong anesthetic could be fatal. On the other hand, how epic would it be to have "He Died Saving the Universe" on his tombstone?

LAST LINE

No matter how many paragraphs you use, your last line should end with a general description of the final conflict and what's at stake for the main character if he or she fails to achieve his or her goal, at least so far as he or she is aware. Using character POV in the book description gives you some room to play with how you present your final conflict and its stakes.

Most books use statement form, laying out the risks and rewards as a statement of fact. "If [the main character] cannot [succeed], he [or she] will [suffer the consequences of failure]."

A few book descriptions end with a question, usually in the form of, "Will [the main character] [succeed], or will he [or she] [suffer the consequences of failure]?"

A third option falls somewhere between these two as far as resolution goes, but it, too, is rarely used. This kind of book description will simply trail off with an ellipsis, leaving the reader to assume at least partial stakes based on context, tone, and genre. "[Main character] must [succeed] or else…"

WORDS, WORDS, WORDS

Y OU HAVE A MAXIMUM OF two hundred words to impress potential readers. You have your ingredients. You have your spices. But what about measuring spoons and brand names? More choices await!

EVOCATIVE LANGUAGE

Word choice is critical when you only have one or two hundred words to convince readers that your book is going to blow their minds. Every one of the words you use needs to pull its weight. If you use flat, boring words, weak verbs, and lots of telling—separating the facts of the story from the action— your description won't let readers expect very much from your book. Strong, accurate verbs, adjectives, and descriptive phrases should paint a clear and exciting image in readers' minds, not only about the content of your book but also about how reading that content will make them feel.

Readers want to be happy with the stories they read, and authors want readers to enjoy their works. Once you've written the book, your only obstacle that remains is selling readers on your story.

GREAT EXPECTATIONS

Because you have so few words with which to sway your potential readers, every one is important. Each one subtly creates an expectation in the readers' minds regarding how much they can expect to enjoy the book. Even after you have chosen how many paragraphs you're going to use and have laid out every sentence, you still have plenty of work to do.

Find your descriptive phrases and words. What does *naïve* seem to say about your female lead? What if you changed it to *innocent*? Would that make her more or less appealing? And what about that final conflict? Is it really *a deadly choice*? Or would it sound better if you called it *the worst mistake of his life*?

The answers depend on what your story actually says—you don't want to mislead your readers—and which genre your story matches. Protagonists should come across as sympathetic but flawed, and antagonists need to be perceived as legitimate threats. Conflict should arouse your readers' curiosity as to how your protagonists will fare at the end.

CAREFUL WORD SELECTION IS KEY

The tone of your book will be reflected in your choice of adjectives. The difference between *haunting* and *reminiscent*, between *girlish* and *innocent*, and a hundred other synonym pairs will affect your readers' perceptions of the tone of your story and the content of your book. Make sure you know the actual definition—the denotation—of every word you use in your book description. But also make sure you are aware of any positive or negative connotations associated with your power words—your gripping, exciting nouns and adjectives—so that you imply what you mean to imply.

Is working with the new boss difficult, or is it challenging? Is Uncle Burt stingy, or is he economical? Does the sexy banker nitpick the details, or is he meticulous? Is the young faerie childish, or is she childlike?

When in doubt, use the dictionary to make sure you understand all possible permutations of your word choice. The last thing you want is for your blurb to imply something incorrect—or worse, hilariously incorrect—about your book. Check your options with the finest of combs to make sure you're using words that give readers the proper impression of the tone of your story.

ADVERBS

Authors regularly hear advice on avoiding adverbs when writing fiction. This guidance also applies to writing book descriptions. Adverbs are useful in the right situations, but too often, inexperienced authors will pair a weak verb with an adverb instead of searching for a stronger, more specific word. Since a single strong word is one less word than a weak verb and its accompanying adverb, seeking out strong, specific language is doubly important when writing a book description. Not only do stronger words make your story pop, but they also save on space. *He gets really angry* doesn't pack nearly the punch that *He rages* does. *She really doesn't like him* feels weak compared to *She despises him*.

WORD REPETITION

Bombastic language comes in all shapes and forms, but because we're writing our description about just one cohesive story, and we're using just the one brain to do it, we often find ourselves using the same superlative word several times during the course of the description. During later edits, make sure to keep your eye out for repeated words. Purposely loading your description with repetition as a hook isn't a good idea.

> "Life whips Garrie out of her rut faster than a hot snake escaping a wagon rut when her sister Margie produces an old Apache treasure map. Margie insists Garrie whip herself into shape before she tackles the great outdoors, though—a sedentary life is no way to get rich, any way you look at it. Newly kitted with a killer six-pack, a fedora, and a bull whip, Garrie joins her sister on the trail of lost gold. But her whip is no match for whip-thin Whip Wilson and his guerilla goons."

GENRE FOCUS

Every genre comes with its own reader expectations. As well as telling your readers what your book is about, your description should assure them that it contains familiar tropes. However, tropes are not clichés. A cliché is something that is used in exactly the same way over and over, until everyone is tired of seeing it, because it never changes. A trope, on the other hand, is a story element that does change, is born afresh with every new book it's used in, and hasn't worn out its welcome because it's so essential to the genre.

Examples of reassuring tropes include the setting itself in genres such as fantasy, historical fiction, and steampunk. Difficulties between romantically attracted characters lie at the heart of every romance novel. Character skill sets are also important in genres such as action thrillers, where we follow a gritty, competent hero as he takes on deadly problems. A trail of cleverly disguised clues in any mystery novel helps the sleuth solve the crime.

GENRE-SPECIFIC LANGUAGE

Every genre has its own buzz words, which are basically linguistic cues to the reader that confirm the book's genre. Romance books may use words like *flush* or *beguiling*, but you probably won't see too much of that in the thriller genre, where they use words such as *riveting* and *questions*. Remember to select your words based on the genre you have written, so that your target audience will recognize your book as belonging to the genre they prefer.

TRIMMING FOR YOUR GENRE

Your first few drafts of your description will likely be far too long. That's perfectly fine. When you trim, however, make sure not to cut out the parts that will appeal most to your target audience. If you've written a murder mystery, you'll want to retain a reference to the (first) body. Your sci-fi book description should mention a hint of your worldbuilding tech, whether in societal advances or cool laser guns. Romance always needs that personal touch: the main character's previous romantic circumstances or current opinion on love.

DON'T GET ATTACHED

Just because you come up with a catchy phrase or line to use in your book description early on doesn't mean it's worth keeping. If you've written a fast-paced technothriller, you don't want to use a description like "deeply soulful rock hound Mark Atwater." Such language will imply that your main character spends a lot of time away from all things technological, perhaps engaging in navel-gazing, which puts him directly at odds with the pacing of your novel and will either confuse or mislead your readers.

Perhaps a phrase from your opening scene jumps out at you, such as "a jog-by coning," where a character slams an ice cream cone into someone's face as she exercises past. Readers would expect such a quirky phrase to reflect a comedic chick-lit novel, or possibly a hilarious cozy mystery caper. But if your book is actually a police procedural with a female lead detective, who was perhaps investigating the ice cream bandit instead of doing the coning herself, then you've completely misled potential readers as to the tone and even the genre of your book.

GENRE SPECIFICS: FLAVORS OF THE MONTH

T HE FOLLOWING ARE EXAMPLE BOOK descriptions for seven public-domain novels belonging to some of literature's most popular genres, in no particular order. The novels' selection for this guide book is based on clear plotwork, popularity, and solid genre standing, though your mileage may vary.

ROMANCE

Often, book descriptions in the traditional romance genre will give one paragraph to the female character, then one to the male character. In addition, they will offer up internal conflict first, frequently belonging to the female character, then the external conflict, which they attach to the male character. Because the female character will almost always be the POV character, it makes sense to give her the internal conflict. In such cases, males' external circumstances are made explicit in the description in order to balance the conflicts within the plot. Alternately, both characters may receive both internal and external conflicts within their respective paragraphs.

Generally, romance-genre book descriptions use a minimum of two paragraphs and a maximum of three.

Here's an example book description for *Pride and Prejudice*, by Jane Austen. Let's look at its basic layout and examine the style, information, and individual word choices.

Tagline: Faults lie in the eye of the beholder.

Elizabeth Bennet suffers from a large, crazy family—four sisters, a mother bent on matchmaking, and a father who's long since retreated into passive cynicism—and a middle-class country life that promises to bore her to death. When young Mr. Bingley moves in nearby and shows interest in Elizabeth's favorite sister, Jane, she finds herself enmeshed in the haughty concerns of the idle rich.

No one has ever been so classless as to mention Fitzwilliam Darcy's prideful character to his face—they're either too genteel or too awed by his vast fortune—until he meets the spirited and clever Elizabeth while visiting Mr. Bingley. Confronted by a darker image of himself than he likes, Mr. Darcy must decide whether to admit fault or cling to his towering pride.

A series of misunderstandings and meddling deceptions keeps Elizabeth and Mr. Darcy apart, until a family crisis strikes the Bennet household. Then she must turn to him for aid, and for the kindness she's never believed he possessed.

The tagline is a play on the well-known saying about beauty, which ties into the older era when this book takes place as well as the central conflict between the two main characters: they don't instantly fall in love, not even close. Instead, they see only each other's faults rather than their true selves. There is also a subtle play on words, where instead of copying the old saying closely with "fault is in the eye of the beholder," we've made it plural, one fault per main character. We switched the weak verb *is* for a stronger verb, *lie* which has the added benefit of being a double entendre. Not only do the faults exist within the characters, but in a way, they deceive the beholders about each other's true natures.

The first paragraph deals with Elizabeth, the main female character in the book. It opens with a short summary of her home life and the struggles she faces there, to show her status quo as the plot begins. Mentioning that her mother is in a matchmaking phase implies that Elizabeth and her sisters are all of marrying age yet still living at home. Her social status is also clarified as middle class. The second sentence leads Elizabeth into conflict by showing that she has gotten far more than she wanted, and she's in over her head with a slice of society she doesn't fully understand. This carries her through the first act of the book, which, as mentioned earlier, is about as far as you should take your book description using specifics.

Strong verbs and evocative language help make Elizabeth's paragraph stand out. Elizabeth suffers from her family instead of simply having one, and her mother is *bent on matchmaking* as opposed to merely enjoying it. Elizabeth's life isn't just boring, it *promises to bore her to death*, implying there is no escape and never will be. And after Bingley shows interest in Jane, Elizabeth doesn't just get drawn into the ways of the idle rich; she becomes *enmeshed*, meaning she couldn't get out if she wanted to. And it's not just their ways but also their *haughty concerns* that enmesh her, implying a fundamental difference between the way Elizabeth sees the world and the way the rich folks view the world, which becomes a significant issue in the book.

This first paragraph summarizes the beginning of the story for Elizabeth, showing where she starts from and the first conflict that draws her into the rest of the story. Because of the specific circumstances at the beginning of this novel, not everything in Elizabeth's paragraph is internal conflict. However, we do show dissatisfaction with her status quo, and as she adapts to new circumstances, she meets with even more frustration as her outlook on life clashes with that of the other characters.

The second paragraph deals with Mr. Darcy. We begin straight away with his status quo, shown to be almost unbearably wealthy and genteel as well as essentially immune to social rebuke. The second part of the first sentence shakes up Mr. Darcy by introducing him to Elizabeth, who challenges his views simply by being herself. She's the first person he's ever met who has called him out, and in the second sentence, we explain that he honestly doesn't know how to handle it. That sets up an impasse between the characters, and the third paragraph will hint at a resolution to that impasse.

Darcy's paragraph begins with a sentence that describes his status: *No one has ever been so classless*. This line gives the impression that, in Darcy's world, such things are simply not done, not to him. The words between the dashes, *they're either too genteel or too awed by his vast fortune*, tuck in a few details to flesh out his circumstances. This section is from his point of view, so when we say *spirited* and *clever*, that is how Darcy sees Elizabeth despite himself. Elizabeth's positive traits are shown with evocative words that have positive connotation for the reader. *Spirited* sounds much better than synonyms like gritty, nervy, sharp, or hyper. And *clever* makes Elizabeth far more appealing than she would be if we called her brainy, cunning, or sly. Most of those words don't give you the romance novel vibe, either. This is why it's so important to spend time looking over specific word choices after you've gotten your basic layout in place. Not only do they need to portray your characters or story the way you want them to, but they also need to fit your genre.

The third paragraph sets up the rest of the novel, showing how the characters struggle with their misunderstandings of each other until a crisis forces them together. Then perhaps they will finally get the chance to truly understand and appreciate each other for the first time. And who doesn't want that kind of happy ending?

When it comes to mentioning the ending of the book, a description should never give away specific details of the plot or the fates of the characters, but it should be packed with as much evocative language as possible in order to make the ending of the book seem so irresistible that readers will have to buy it immediately in order to find out what happens. Thus, we have a *family crisis*, which is nonspecific as far as the plot is concerned, yet most of us have experienced at least one of those during our lifetimes, so most readers will know how wrenching they can be to endure, even with loved ones to lean on. And that family crisis doesn't just happen—it *strikes*, implying a sudden and unexpected occurrence.

The final paragraph doesn't mention the outcome of Elizabeth going to Mr. Darcy for help, and it shouldn't. The reader needs to buy the book to find out what happens. It's just like poker, when you have to pay to see another player's cards. And since this is a romantic novel, it's pretty well understood that the trope of the happy ending will ensure that, some way or another, Elizabeth and Mr. Darcy end up together. But holding back the exact circumstances of that happy ending is vital to catching the reader's interest.

FOR GENRES THAT ARE PART ROMANCE AND PART SOMETHING ELSE

Genres such as romantic suspense, romantic fantasy, romantic sci-fi, romantic thriller, and so forth contain plots formed primarily of the second listed genre, with a romantic tone throughout the book. If your book falls into this category, you can emphasize the romantic angle for your readers by mentioning the female in one paragraph and the male in another. Since that is a common pattern in romance genre book descriptions, it will be a visual cue to your readers that your book definitely claims romance as its secondary genre.

MYSTERY/SUSPENSE

Stories of this genre often begin with a trigger event such as a death, disappearance, or some other kind of crime. As a general rule, the initial crime takes place during the first one hundred pages. So the information about this external conflict often appears first in book descriptions for this genre, with the second paragraph relating internal conflict for the main character.

These genres and their subgenres—cozy mystery, technothriller, police procedural, and so on—all contain a common element that's essential to the reader's satisfaction: the puzzle. Make sure you include, and even emphasize, an aspect of that puzzle in your description. What's the coolest part? The arrogant serial killer and his quirky death poses? A suspicious neighbor who always seems to be standing over the body? A ticking clock that will signal a hostage's death?

Though books within these genres contain some kind of puzzle, your specific puzzle is what makes your book stand out. Draw attention to that, and you'll promise readers a unique read within a genre that interests them.

Here's an example book description for *A Study in Scarlet* by Sir Arthur Conan Doyle. Let's look at its basic layout and examine the style, information, and individual word choices.

Tagline: Dedication has a dark side.

Dr. John Watson, invalided home from the war in Afghanistan, lands a flatmate, Sherlock Holmes, who's a genius at chemistry, anatomy, and British law but is woefully ignorant of such trifles as the earth's orbiting of the sun. So when Scotland Yard asks for Holmes's help with a baffling death, Watson's pretty sure he's the only one who isn't crazy.

When Holmes claims he's already deduced the killer from seemingly random clues, Watson's concerns grow. His worries seem validated when Holmes's scheme to reveal the killer fails entirely because he can't even keep track of an elderly woman in a four-wheeler cab. But Holmes has more than enough faith in himself for the both of them.

In order to catch the wily murderer, Holmes must lay a clever trap that endangers both his life and Watson's, and if Watson manages to survive, he will never be the same.

This tagline has a double meaning, for both Sherlock Holmes and the villain he is chasing. Holmes is highly intelligent, but in some ways, his life is unbalanced as a result of his dedication to detection. As readers discover the full plot, they'll realize that the tagline also applies to the years of work the villain has put into his vengeful scheme. Taglines usually do best when they can mean more than one thing or when their meaning evokes a distinct emotional reaction without giving plot specifics.

The first part of the first sentence in the first paragraph sums up who Watson is. He's a doctor, he's a soldier, and he's wounded, so he can't participate in the war anymore. That sums up how someone like him ends up in London, away from his primary field of expertise. *Invalided home* is a military term used widely during the era when the book is set, and it simply means a soldier has been too wounded to continue serving in the military and thus has been sent back to his home country. In just a few words, we've set Watson's character in place and time. Next, we move on to the rest of his status quo: he has a new flatmate. The term is distinctly British, which tells readers which country the story takes place in.

Then we move on to more detail about this flatmate. Watson has just met the man and doesn't really understand him very well yet, but Watson's made some observations, and he's worried that this guy who claims to be a genius might be just a crackpot. This reflects Watson's internal conflict. Yet the plot moves on when Scotland Yard enters the scene and enlists Sherlock's help. This adds more internal conflict for Watson. Is he wrong about Sherlock, or is Scotland Yard, the preeminent investigative force in England, wrong? Since this is a mystery book, that question is absolutely begging to be answered, but the description isn't going to give the reader that satisfaction.

The word choice in the first paragraph is a combination of setting the scene and use of evocative language. Such terms as *invalided home*, *flatmate*, *British law*, and *Scotland Yard* help to anchor the story's era in England. The contrast of *genius* with *woefully ignorant* shows Watson's conflicting opinions on Sherlock's character. And when the police authority runs up against a *baffling death*, that hints at the complexity of the case Sherlock and Watson will take on.

The second paragraph moves to the investigation phase, where Watson follows Sherlock's lead despite his misgivings. Sherlock isn't stopping long enough to explain himself, so Watson, who considers himself a reasonably intelligent man, still isn't sure Sherlock is on the right trail. Then a seemingly easy task blows up in Sherlock's face. How hard is it to track an old woman through the city? Well, that depends, doesn't it? This is a mystery, and anything and everything we put in a mystery book's description can be considered a clue. Readers are going to know by the sheer fact that we mention how this old woman eluded Sherlock that there must be more to her escape than meets the eye. And they won't be wrong. Adding a clue that seems to support Watson's doubt in Sherlock—when in fact, it's merely upping the ante as to what's at stake for Sherlock and Watson—will entice the reader to read the book in order to discover the full truth. The final line in the second paragraph refers to Sherlock's character, offering reassurance to the reader that they aren't reading a book about an idiot while giving Watson some more internal conflict to deal with.

The language of doubt continues in the second paragraph, with words such as *claims* and *seemingly random*. Watson receives such language as *validated*, while Sherlock is brought even lower with *fails entirely*. The final line reverses the trend, though, setting up for the final conflict with the words *more than enough faith*.

The final paragraph deals with the final conflict in the book. Sherlock goes to an extreme in order to prove that he's right and that he knows who the killer is. Watson hasn't run away yet, despite his doubts, implying that he is coming around to Sherlock's way of dealing with the world and its problems. But Sherlock's plan holds a real risk of death, and the final line implies, without using specifics, that Watson will most likely survive but will be irrevocably changed by this first case with Sherlock Holmes. Does that mean he will be wounded again? Will he turn against Sherlock for risking Watson's life, or perhaps will he become a slavish worshiper at the altar of Holmes's genius? Curious, mystery-solving minds want to know!

Hinting that a character will be forever changed by a final conflict is always a fun draw for readers. We go through our lives learning lessons, gaining scars, and hopefully picking up some wisdom from the adventures and struggles we deal with, and readers find it realistic and appealing when fictional characters do the same.

SPECULATIVE FICTION

If your speculative fiction novel involves significant worldbuilding—such as with creating a secondary world, a galaxy, an alternate universe, magic systems, an alternate reality on Earth, or a futuristic or postapocalyptic Earth—you will need to frame your scenario early in your description so your readers understand your characters, your conflict, and what's at stake. Make sure you work in some words that detail the setting as early in the description as you can, but avoid at all costs such clichéd phrases as "In a world where…" That's best left to the voice-overs for movie trailers.

Speculative fiction settings are a significant portion of the reason readers are drawn to the genre in the first place. They love to see a little bit of the familiar mixed and matched with new and brain-tingling concepts: new cultures, rules, tech, magic, creatures, and dangers. When you are framing your scenario, be sure to use vivid, eye-catching language that makes your setting as appealing as possible. The greatest compliment such books receive is when readers say they desperately wish they could climb through the pages and live there. Your description can serve as an invitation to visit.

Here's an example book description for *20,000 Leagues under the Sea* by Jules Verne. Let's look at its basic layout and examine the style, information, and individual word choices.

Tagline: Hearts will sink.

As a new era of invention and exploration dawns across the civilized world, a powerful threat rises from the depths of the sea. Its attacks are far from random—and impossible to stop. Irate nations demand the deadly behemoth be killed, and skeptical marine biologist Professor Aronnax is invited to join the seaborne hunt.

The crew's assault on the elusive beast goes disastrously wrong, and Aronnax, his assistant, and Ned Land, an independent-minded sailor, are captured by a tortured genius known only as Captain Nemo, whose sea monster is a phenomenon far more incredible and dangerous than anything Aronnax could have imagined. Though their all-too-human captor shares his love of the undersea and his astonishing technological innovations with his prisoners, Nemo keeps his past as secret as his motives.

Despite sharing Nemo's scientific proclivities, Aronnax finds his loyalties pushed to the breaking point when dark and painful truths surface regarding the captain's intentions. Caught in a maelstrom of doubt, sympathy, and horror, Aronnax must choose between a dream and a nightmare, between a golden future and the man who invented it.

Our tagline is another play on words. It implies something sad or horrific will occur during the course of the plot, which ties in with many science fiction and postapocalyptic undercurrents: the technology we create only fuels the dark side of humanity. In addition, saying that hearts will sink is a nod to the submarine *Nautilus*, which pulls our heroes into a dark world below.

The first paragraph begins with a line that sets the scene for the story world's level of technological advancement. It also contrasts events happening on land with those happening in the sea, implying that as far as this novel's worldview is concerned, the sea is a wild, untamed mass of emotion compared to the logic and progress on terra firma. The next line shows that the threat from the sea is not only powerful but also actively attacking, setting up initial conflict for the story. The final line introduces our main protagonist, Professor Aronnax, and contrasts him as a man of intelligence against the irate nations who thought that hiring a marine biologist was the solution to their problems. Usually, we want to name our protagonist no later than the second sentence, but in this case, worldbuilding takes precedence, and Aronnax is still named in the first paragraph.

In the novel, Aronnax is indeed skeptical that such a large biological creature could exist without prior discovery. However, lives are at stake, and as a man of conscience, he agrees to go on the expedition, allowing for the admittedly remote possibility that he is wrong. All this character information is summed up in the description by the phrase *skeptical marine biologist*, which shows him to be a thinking man of science.

Language in the first paragraph opens with the dawn of a new era, the concept of which heavily influences the book's tone. Not only is the book full of scientific discoveries, but it also pushes the boundaries of possibility with that bright, shiny "everything is possible for he who dares to think it" mentality. Since that theme is such a strong part of the book, it's important to set that tone in the reader's mind early in the description, as well. The land is contrasted with the sea, and directional influence also comes into play. Science and invention are shown to expand *across*, showing all men to be equally competent, while the threat from the sea *rises* from below. If we break out a little psychology here, we could tie that into the forebrain and hindbrain, with one representing social awareness and intellect, and the other our darkest, deepest emotional instincts and impulses. If you have this kind of symbolism in your book, work it into the description with symbolic language and detail so readers will be, on at least a subconscious level, prepared for those concepts before they even begin reading.

The second paragraph outlines the initial conflict and its aftermath, leading the characters into the rest of the plot. Aronnax has already been introduced, and his assistant very much takes his side during the plot, but Ned Land, the harpooner from the expedition who was captured with them, is a constant source of contradiction and escape attempts while aboard the *Nautilus*. Also, his last name is Land, and that's where he's constantly trying to get back to: the lands of civilization and safety. An author might choose not to mention everyone's name in a collection of major characters due to word count constraints, but in this case, Ned's last name has a double meaning, so drawing the reader's attention to it, even briefly, will give a small boost to the conflicts promised within the plot.

The rest of the paragraph introduces and details Captain Nemo. We contrast him, as *all-too-human*, with the *sea monster* that belongs to him and touch on his character by calling him a *tortured genius* with secrets. By saying that Nemo *shares* with his captives, we show that he's capable of generosity, though since he doesn't free his captives, we make sure his morality remains distinctly in the gray area.

Word choices in the second paragraph are aimed at ramping up the sense of conflict. The crew doesn't simply attack what they think is a sea monster; they *assault* it. And when they fail, they don't simply fail. We employ the word *disastrously*.

Since the sea monster's true form as a submarine is a big mystery toward the beginning of the novel, we don't reveal it in the description, but we do hint that it is not what it seems to be by using the word *phenomenon*. That word is often applied to naturally occurring events or creatures, but since the *Nautilus* is the only creation of its kind, it's more of a technological phenomenon. Because the book deals with what was cutting-edge technology at the time of its publication, this paragraph is also seasoned with power words such as *incredible*, *dangerous*, and *astonishing*.

In the last paragraph, we draw toward the foggy outline of the final conflict without revealing its true nature to the reader. Aronnax learns some of Nemo's secrets, and he is forced to choose between the two sides of Nemo's nature: a scientific love of the sea and a hatred of the dark side of humankind, which has, unfortunately, seeped into Nemo, as well. We use the word *maelstrom* to show a nautical relation with the multiple internal conflicts Aronnax is battling as he struggles with his decision.

In the final sentence, parallels show a fuller metaphor for the two sides of the struggle. The dream pairs with a golden future, representing the best of humanity and our ability to shape our world with our intellect. The nightmare, on the other hand, pairs with Nemo's dark side and how he uses his magnificent technology to destroy. These final phrases set up and reinforce what's at stake for Aronnax and, by extension, what's at stake for the rest of civilization. The bigger the stakes, the more exciting that final conflict will be, so referring to the advancement of mankind as a metaphor for one of Aronnax's choices brings the whole world into play.

HISTORICAL FICTION

Historical fiction covers every era in human history and might even run right up to the end of the last millennium, depending on whom you ask. Most people define historical fiction for themselves as any story that took place before they were born.

Books in this genre often cross with a secondary genre in order to tell a story. Such popular historical fiction genres include war novels, medieval English and European romances, tales of pirate adventure, romance, and anything that centers around a critical point of interest in history. But really, just about anything goes, as long as you tell it appealingly.

Some worldbuilding is required with any historical fiction description, in order to cement the time and place of the story, and any significance thereof, in the reader's mind. Small details and turns of phrase are generally sufficient for this task. Giant swaths of telling (see *Don't get facty* in the next section) use far too many words and can come across like a history book. If readers expect to read a novel but find they purchased a history book instead, they're going to walk away, possibly after leaving a grumpy review. Remember that your description serves as a tiny mirror for the whole of your novel. If you pack it with dates, names, places, and other overt historical details, readers will assume that your entire novel will be like that, and they'll probably pass. Pick out the universal details of your story and focus on those. Why is your story so appealing after so much time has passed? Tell us about that and sprinkle a little historical-detail spice here and there, and you'll have readers eating out of the palm of your hand.

Here's an example book description for *Les Miserables* by Victor Hugo. Let's look at its basic layout and examine the style, information, and individual word choices.

Tagline: Earn your fate.

Released in Digne, France, after nineteen years in the galleys for an act that should never have been considered a crime, Jean Valjean is a bitter, angry man. But when the local bishop unexpectedly forgives him for stealing some precious silver, Valjean alters his identity and dedicates himself to changing his ways. His past catches up with him, however, when his own act of mercy reveals his formidable strength to Inspector Javert, who remembers Valjean as one of the convicts he guarded.

Valjean's and Javert's fates link when they clash over the lot of a desperate prostitute named Fantine. Valjean rescues Fantine's daughter, Cosette, and raises her as his own, but the harsh inspector only sees a convict masquerading as a law-abiding citizen and chooses a path of strict justice, determined to hunt him down.

As the years pass, Valjean escapes Javert time and again, but raising a beautiful young daughter in nineteenth-century Paris is a daunting task made dangerous against the backdrop of anti-Orléanist civil unrest that threatens to consume the city. As the nets of loyalty, destiny, and insurrection close around him and the specter of his nemesis draws near once more, Valjean realizes he could never have run forever.

Our tagline is short, but it employs one of the main themes in the book: that the people we choose to be determine the rewards we receive in life, no matter by which means. The main character, Valjean, is a lowly fellow, but at the beginning of the story, he decides to become a better person, and his future begins to look up. In contrast, the main villain, Javert, continually clings to his letter-of-the-law interpretation of life, and as a result, his character never really grows. Each man's final fate seems to be a karmic reward for the kind of man he was during his life.

In addition, *earn* has a positive connotation, implying room for redemption. *Fate* carries both positive and negative connotations, depending on which major character the reader applies it to. We employed *fate* as an equivalent to *doom* in regard to Javert's fate, but we also want readers to see the positive side of fate, which is *destiny*, as it applies to Valjean.

Our first paragraph opens with a sentence that sets up an environment of injustice: Valjean has done something that got him in trouble but shouldn't have, implying that justice in his day and age is far from fair. This will help readers expect plenty of conflicts in which they should obviously feel sympathy for only Valjean. The story carries a sense of black and white. The length of Valjean's punishment also alludes to the unfairness of the time, so it is a good supporting detail to include. And finally, Valjean's character is given as *bitter* and *angry*. These are negative traits, to be sure. But it's necessary to show where he begins his journey, so that when he makes his decision to change, readers will understand what he's trying to move away from within himself.

The next sentence shows the event that triggers Valjean's change of heart: he's unexpectedly forgiven for a crime against a holy man. He did a pretty terrible thing, yet he wasn't punished. Seeing a different path open up in front of him, he takes it. Most plots contain at least one early trigger, and it's important to mention it in your description to add believability and specificity to the impetus for your story.

The final sentence in the first paragraph informs the reader that Valjean's journey will not be an easy one, and it introduces the main villain, Javert, who is a good chunk of the reason why Valjean's journey will be difficult. It shows that Valjean is now being merciful, but Javert is not. This sets up the prime difference between the men and their internal source of conflict, right at the start.

The language used at the beginning of this historical fiction description needs to evoke that genre. This is accomplished through mentioning France in the first sentence, along with the fact that prisoners are punished by making them rot in galleys for years on end—a punishment that definitely places this story in the past.

The second paragraph brings protagonist and antagonist together, further contrasting their natures as they choose different reactions to a single event. The book is flooded with opportunities to choose one way or the other, so contrasting the way these two characters react, showing the choices they make early on, lets the reader see the beginning of each of their paths. Again, though, we want to make sure we don't give away anything past the first third or so of the book. This book is long, so we have a lot to work with, but we still don't want to give away anything specific in the middle or the end.

To that end, the description leaves out vast swaths of minor characters. In general, you don't want to put any subplots in your description, only the main plot. All the side issues that our main hero and villain get up to need to remain surprises for the readers simply because there is no room to tell readers about this full plot and all those little ones in two hundred words or so.

The wording in the second paragraph purposely continues with the tone of the book. The two men clash, good and evil, and the word *link* evokes chains and implies that they cannot escape one another. Their battle takes on an eternal quality. The prostitute isn't saucy or catty; she's *desperate*. And while Valjean proves his heroism by rescuing a helpless child, Inspector Javert gets words like *harsh* and *strict*. He's *determined to hunt him down*, rather than something more positive like *determined to bring him to justice*. He feels something darker, something more personal. When you hunt something down, you treat it like prey, like an animal—something less than your equal. We use this phrase to describe Javert's attitude toward Valjean so that the character's evil intent will be reinforced in readers' minds.

The final paragraph skips ahead toward the final conflict of the novel and spices itself with a few more historical terms to help cement the era and flavor of the story. *Nineteenth-century France* and *anti-Orléanist civil unrest* evoke not only the time period but also the political nature of the conflict among the common people, which serves as the backdrop for Valjean's story. And we used just five words.

The first sentence allows time to pass and gives away only that Javert has not stopped hunting Valjean over the years while Valjean continues to be merciful to the young girl he rescued. This shows readers that both men are still choosing to embody the same character they chose. And the final sentence draws several plot lines together from the book, without giving specifics: *loyalty*, *destiny*, and *insurrection*. Power words often come in twos or threes in the final paragraph of your book description, embodying high-concept ideas that will lure readers to buy your book.

Destiny is a huge part of this book, and we've been planting it in readers' minds since the tagline. It is bookended by the positive loyalty and the negative insurrection, allowing a bit of uncertainty to enter into the readers' minds as to whether *destiny* will be good or bad, rather like *fate*. The ending is left vague, implying indirectly that Javert finally catches Valjean, but as any book lover knows, the last line of a book description is never a guarantee of accuracy. Writers are a sneaky lot, and most of the time, any facts that seem certain at the end of a book description mean something else entirely once you read the plot.

The wording in the final paragraph is meant to make the stakes seem as high as possible. Valjean's daughter is both young and beautiful, and his task of raising her is not only daunting but also quite dangerous. The civil unrest isn't a mere irritant—it *threatens to consume*. The plot lines that draw around Valjean are described as nets, which trap him, rather than something more benign, like threads in a tapestry. Javert has become metaphorically superhuman, paranormal, like an inescapable nemesis, so we use the word *specter* to show his continual, haunting presence in the background of Valjean's life.

Historical fiction involves stories that are consciously set in a different era than our own, so the task with any book description for this genre is to describe bygone events in such a way that universal concepts shine through for the reader, making an instant connection they can easily identify with.

YOUNG ADULT

Young adult books are not a genre but rather books aimed at an age-defined target audience. YA books inhabit every genre but are written to appeal to a younger audience by emphasizing storylines, character traits, plots, values, and themes that appeal more strongly to them. Generally, YA book descriptions are shorter and less complex, rarely exceeding two paragraphs in length, which reflects a tendency toward more straightforward plots.

Sentence length is often simpler and shorter, as well, simply because there can be less critical information to impart in order to understand the story's basis. That leaves more opportunity for short and powerful sentences that deliver a single, important concept. That's not to say we want to use a bunch of really short, really repetitive sentences in a row. We don't. Sentence structure should be varied and vivid in any book description, no matter your target audience. Writing a book for a certain audience then insinuating they're too stupid to understand it sends decidedly mixed signals.

Because YA novels come in all sizes, colors, and shapes, it's important that you clearly convey the tone and genre of your story in your description.

Here's an example book description for the YA coming-of-age novel *Anne of Green Gables* by Lucy Maud Montgomery. Let's look at its basic layout and examine the style, information, and individual word choices.

> *Tagline: Home is where they love you anyway.*
>
> *Eleven-year-old Anne Shirley never asked to be an orphan. She definitely didn't ask for red hair. When she's mistakenly sent to an island farm whose owners asked for a boy, Marilla and her brother, Matthew, decide to keep her anyway. Ruled by romantic ideals and poetic passions, Anne soon manages to insult the town's matriarch, make an enemy of the charismatic Gilbert Blythe, and accidentally get her best friend, Diana, drunk.*
>
> *As the years pass, Anne dives wholeheartedly into well-intentioned misadventure and scholastic competition with her bitter rival, Gilbert. But as she stands on the cusp of a bright, hard-earned future, tragedy strikes, and neither Anne nor the quiet island town of Avonlea will ever be the same.*

Our tagline here references that "home is where you find it" vibe. It implies the character who's going to find this home won't be perfect but will still be accepted. That sort of reassurance sets a positive tone in this YA book.

The YA genre can have protagonists with ages that range from preteen to late teen. Any one of us can look back on our growth and development during those years of our own lives and realize that we were very different at the beginning of that time period than we were at the end. That makes it important to set the age or maturity level for your YA character early in the description, so readers will get a feel for the range of events that the main character might encounter during the plot. In this case, since Anne is so young and is not living at home, we've simply gone with her age. There is no love interest, since she's too young for that, and she has no conflict with her parents to show that she's still living at home. A YA character's age is an easy default that your readers are very comfortable seeing.

The first two sentences use a tone that shows Anne isn't getting the best start in life, according to her. She's an orphan, and on top of that, her hair is red. Horrors! But then she catches a break, and the next sentence introduces the authority figures who accept her. We've also made the distinction that the two people running the farm are not a married couple, as most would assume. The final sentence lets Anne loose, showing her character and how she still doesn't really fit in, while introducing two more major characters who play important roles in the plot: rival Gilbert and bestie Diana.

Word choice in the first paragraph is aimed at showing Anne as a misfit. The *definitely* shows that she really does not care for her hair color. And she can't even get adopted properly, being *mistakenly sent*. Once she's in Avonlea, we show her being a little out of control by saying she is *ruled by* her ideals and passions. She doesn't intend to cause trouble, so we use the words *manages to* and *accidentally* to describe the hijinks in which she finds herself.

The last paragraph summarizes events that take place during the middle and end of the book. Since the book covers several years of Anne's life, it's important to let readers know to expect such. There's a big difference between a book whose plot covers a few weeks and one with a coming-of-age theme that spans a character's entire adolescence. Readers will want to know which one they're getting.

During the book, Anne's character grows but doesn't change. She merely finds new avenues in which to be herself, shown in the description by her continued good intentions and occasional poor judgment. And then we come to the final conflict, in which it's apparent that Anne has learned to apply herself to practical things and has earned herself a chance at a great future. But reality intrudes in a devastating manner, affecting Anne personally and threatening that future. What's an imaginative girl to do with a bad dose of reality? Has her character matured enough to allow her to handle this tragedy? Readers have only one way to find out.

Anne's no slacker. She *dives wholeheartedly* into everything she does. She's no slouch, either, being capable of *scholastic competition* with her rival for years. And who can fault her for a little *well-intentioned misadventure*? She sounds adorable. In the story, Anne sees what she thinks her future will be, but before she can claim it, the tragedy occurs, so we go with *as she stands on the cusp* to show that she is still in a sort of transition zone. That's the best time to strike, when the character still has options, even if they aren't good ones. And that tragedy doesn't just show up—it *strikes*. It's a sudden event, forcing her to reevaluate where she stands. The last part of the last line also implies that Anne isn't the only one affected by the tragedy. The community of Avonlea will have to adjust to something difficult, as well. This integrates Anne into the community at last, as everyone deals with the same circumstances, and shows that, in a way, Anne has finally come home.

HORROR

The job of any horror novel is to let readers vicariously experience danger while safely sitting on their couch or huddling under their covers with a flashlight. The genre lets us explore the darkest parts of our own existence, plumb our deepest fears, and feel that delicious tingle of fear down our spines as we let our imaginations run rampant.

Generally, horror novels take place on Earth, though that's by no means a hard rule. Because the average horror novel's setting is going to be at least vaguely familiar to the reader, there is usually little worldbuilding required, aside from the basic description of setting, character, and conflict. This gives horror novel descriptions the option of running a little shorter than the ones of some other genres.

An added benefit to a shorter horror description is the element of mystery. Sometimes, horror characters experience trepidation because they don't yet understand what they're up against. It's no fun if we ruin that sensation for the readers by giving away too much in the description.

Here's an example book description for *Dracula* by Bram Stoker. Let's look at its basic layout and examine the style, information, and individual word choices.

A DARK LINEAGE WITH ANCIENT ROOTS

English lawyer Jonathan Harker's mission is simple: meet a reclusive count in his cliffside castle in Eastern Europe to finalize a real estate transfer. But once Harker arrives, the noctiphilic Dracula refuses to let him leave. Desperate to escape, Harker encounters seductive horrors his logical, reasoning mind can't accept. He manages to flee, but with his sanity in tatters.

A SIREN CALL OF NEW BLOOD

Shortly after a ghost ship runs aground on the English shore, Harker's fiancée, Mina, sees a dark turn in her friend Lucy's behavior. At the nearby sanitarium, Dr. Seward observes the same in his most interesting patient. As Lucy worsens, Dr. Seward sends for Van Helsing, an occult-disease expert. Van Helsing's diagnosis of Lucy is far worse than death: she is transforming into the same sort of wanton monster that attacked her.

A VIOLENT CLASH OF NATURES

Drawn together by frantic desperation, these unlikely allies join forces in a daring bid to destroy the powerful vampire Dracula before his seductive, destructive reach grows too horrific to defeat.

Instead of a tagline, we went with shoutlines for *Dracula*. Including them before each paragraph allows us to essentially give each paragraph its own tagline. Considering this book's two distinct settings—Transylvania and

England—and that entirely different parts of the story take place in each, it's acceptable to use repeated separation. This reflects the idea that the story is like books within a book, but in a condensed, description form.

Our first shoutline reflects Transylvania and Dracula's characters. Our villain is more than a mere mortal. We want him to be perceived as a force of nature, and an evil one at that. Using *ancient roots* helps establish Dracula as a permanent entity.

The first paragraph begins by introducing our main character, Jonathan Harker. Here, as with several other examples, we tuck a few evocative description words before his name in the shorthand of character introduction. The impression of a journey is created with the description of Harker's mission: we have described him as English, yet he is headed for Eastern Europe. He'll clearly be out of his element.

The description delves deeper into Harker's character when we contrast the evil he encounters with his logical approach to life. This conflict forms the basis of the novel itself: how reasoning and logic react when they encounter an unreasoning, evil id. Essentially, this book pits the two halves of humanity against each other and sits back to see who wins. Working such a heavily embedded theme into explicit detail in the description will help prepare readers for its omnipresence in the text.

Harker's encounter with Dracula begins offhandedly, when he perceives the count to be just another client. Soon, he realizes he is not free to leave the castle, bringing that first twist, that first rising conflict, into existence. That's a great way to end the first paragraph of any book description.

Word choice in the first paragraph reflects the theme of the book, using both very positive and very negative connotation for Harker and Dracula, respectively. Dracula goes from *reclusive* to *noctiphilic*, then he *refuses* Harker's requests to leave, forcing Harker to endure *seductive horrors*. Harker, meanwhile, begins with a *simple mission*, which devolves too quickly for his *logical, reasoning mind*, leaving him *desperate*. Eventually, our hero, though finally free, has *his sanity in tatters*. Basically, Dracula's naughty evil wears down Harker's brain. For a guy who considers himself an intellectual, that's horrific indeed.

Our second shoutline and paragraph shift to the second major location, England. Siren calls are notoriously irresistible, which refers to those seductive horrors from the first paragraph. The double entendre of *new blood* refers not only to Dracula's fresh menu items but also to a swath of new characters for the reader to follow. So, not only are we saying that Dracula's about to break into a new buffet, we're also intimating to the reader that this next part of the story is going to be exciting and impossible to put down.

The first sentence of this paragraph introduces Mina and Lucy and creates a connection between them and Harker for continuity. It also employs a ghost ship as a method of bringing conflict, which continues the supernatural theme. Dr. Seward and Van Helsing are introduced in the next two sentences, as well. With these new characters, we're showing a range of relationships and expertise. Mina is a love interest, while Dr. Seward works at a sanitarium, and Van Helsing is an expert on occult diseases. Showing the men's skill sets enables the reader to expect a high level of competency from them. Yet these characters are already forced to play catch-up with the villain, since Lucy has already been struck down, and Van Helsing cannot cure her.

Dracula's movements are not explicitly shown in this paragraph because supernatural creatures need to remain mysterious. We merely imply that Dracula was aboard that ghost ship, and we leave readers to assume that he is the cause of Lucy's ailment, without detailing how any of that came about. The longer we can leave him in shadow and mystery, the more readers will make up their own psychological horrors about him, and the more they will enjoy the story. We leave it to the book to fully reveal Dracula's abilities and character.

Word choice in the second paragraph continues to amplify the inherent differences between logical people and emotional evil. On Dracula's side of the argument, we mention a *ghost ship*, a *dark turn*, and *occult disease* and use phrases like *far worse than death* and *the wanton monster*. For the good guys—one of whom can boast the term *expert*—we use such phrases as *sanitarium*, *most interesting patient*, and *diagnosis*. The *most interesting patient* is a handy phrase, characterizing Dr. Seward as a critical thinker who sees mysteries as things to be studied, not feared.

At this point in the description, Dracula has all the wins in his column. The heroes have lost twice so far, but there's still time for them to eke out a victory. The third shoutline and final paragraph hint at this final conflict. This final shoutline explicitly addresses good and evil nature and implies actual battle, which is always fun. Everyone loves to see a seemingly unstoppable evil get its comeuppance. The paragraph itself merely says that all our characters draw together, without ruining exactly how that comes about or even whether they succeed. Clearly, Lucy's life is on the line, but far more is at stake. However, that is also left vague. Could Dracula be taking over the world? We don't know! We'd better read to find out.

As this plot drags our heroes so far down before giving them the opportunity to strike back, this final paragraph functions like a rubber band stretched almost too far before rebounding quickly in order to show how desperate the characters are at this point in the story.

Because of the violence, the action, and the constant presence of the good vs. evil theme, word repetition was a significant challenge to avoid for this book description. How many times can you say horror, evil, dark, monster, or desperate when describing the plot of *Dracula*? Just once apiece, really. With such a stark theme to this book, all these words are applicable power words, but it's vital to avoid using them more than once. And beware of words that show up in more than one form. For example, we should avoid using both *desperate* and *desperation.* With so few words, why use the same one three times, when you can change two of them and squeeze even more power into your description?

Standard advice is to shun the thesaurus when writing a book, but when you're faced with the challenge of avoiding word repetition, it can be a handy tool. Just make absolutely certain you understand the exact definition of every word you look up so as to avoid accidentally implying something incorrect.

ACTION/ADVENTURE

Action/adventure books generally come with a fast pace and a lot of, well, action. What happens is often more critical to the story than whom it happens to. A strong main character is essential for stories in this genre, since the character will be put under significant stress, repeatedly and from various sources, during the course of the plot. Readers will need to trust that such a hero can carry them to the end, so painting your main character in strong, bold colors is a big part of gaining your readers' trust that you can tell a good story.

Because plots in this genre rely so heavily on fast-paced events, strong verbs and power words are essential in description. While women make up the vast majority of book lovers, this genre is often a haven for male readers. Subtlety will get you nowhere. Conflict and action drive adventure stores, so they should dominate your description as well.

Here's an example book description for *The Count of Monte Cristo* by Alexandre Dumas. Let's look at its basic layout and examine the style, information, and individual word choices.

Tagline: Vengeance is a wronged man's right.

Captain Edmund Dantès's life is looking up—a new promotion and his upcoming nuptials—until his future is hijacked by an unlikely alliance. Torn from his beloved Mercédès on the eve of their wedding and accused of a treason he never committed, Dantès is imprisoned without trial, and his captors spread the lie of his death.

Rage and despair drive Dantès to the brink of suicide, but he serendipitously meets another prisoner, whose escape tunnel takes a wrong turn into Dantès's seaside cell. Abbé Faria, a wealthy political prisoner and philosopher, instructs Dantès in the ways of arts and science as they plot their freedom.

When an unforeseen opportunity for escape plunges Dantès back into civilization, he arms himself with the knowledge and the means to exact his revenge against his conspirators, who have risen in the world during his unjust imprisonment. But rage over their unpunished actions still burns within him, and his revenge on the guilty may spark tragic consequences for the innocent.

Our tagline oozes manliness and a thirst for justice. It portrays our main character's belief that he has every right to extract what he feels is fair from those who have hurt him. It also employs a handy word pair—*wronged* and *right*—that makes readers appreciate balance, subtly tipping their scales in agreement with our main character.

Our first paragraph opens with a one-word categorization for our main character: captain. We add that he's been promoted and is getting married, placing him squarely in the competent-and-attractive-dude category that befits so many action/adventure protagonists. But this is a fast-paced adventure, so we don't waste any time getting to that first rising conflict. The end of the first sentence turns Dantès's world on its ear and shows the conspiracy to be from an unexpected quarter. Not even the best heroes can prepare for every eventuality, but we want to make it clear that there was no way he could have expected this, so his integrity as a hero remains intact. Two equally terrible things happen as a result of this sudden betrayal, and both are equally devastating. He loses his bride and his freedom. Then things get really bad. Because his conspirators want to hide evidence of their crime, they cheat him out of due process and basically lock him away to die in obscurity. That's a pretty difficult obstacle to overcome, so we want to make explicit how dire Dantès's circumstances are, so that his return will appear suitably awesome. Anytime you want to horribly victimize one of your characters so that his or her comeback can be epic, that putdown needs to show up in your description.

Word choice in the first paragraph focuses on action and events. When Dantès's life is *looking up*, it implies he's finally achieving some milestones in his life. But then *his future is hijacked by an unlikely alliance*. This once again makes it clear that he couldn't have seen this coming. *Hijacked* implies a sudden attack, as well, meaning he had no time to prepare a proper defense. Then our poor hero is *torn*, *accused*, and finally *imprisoned*. We saved two words by using *imprisoned* instead of *thrown into prison*, too. Look for anything to trim the word count while still retaining clarity.

Succinct word usage also shows up in the last part of the last sentence, where *his captors spread the lie of his death*. This wording shows they know it's a lie, and they purposely tell everyone, cementing them as nefarious, and this phrasing comes in at several words fewer than something like *his captors tell everyone he's dead, though they know he isn't.*

The second paragraph details a new phase for Dantès's character. At first, he can't find a way out, and he reacts poorly to his helplessness. It's important to show this low point, as well, because he rebounds from it, too. His mentor character, Abbé Faria, enters the plot as a chance encounter, but at the same time, the method of their meeting shows Faria to be a resourceful man. The paragraph concludes with the two characters colluding and Dantès improving himself so as to rise to the challenge he expects to encounter when he escapes: avenging himself. We show him planning ahead—he's a resourceful character, as well, who knows what to do when an opportunity lands in his lap.

Word choice in the second paragraph reflects the sharp descent and rise of Dantès's prospects as he hits bottom and rebounds. It's critical that the reader understand how bitter Dantès became before he found an avenue of hope. Basically, we are foreshadowing the final paragraph with this information here. So we use terms like *rage and despair* and *brink of suicide* to make that low point clear to the readers. Then we turn the corner and use terms with hopeful and positive connotations like *serendipitously* and *escape*. We include Faria's characteristics of being a *wealthy political prisoner and philosopher* who is knowledgeable about *arts and science* as future tools for Dantès's use, and finally, we use *freedom*. Dantès has a goal now, and he's chasing it hard.

The final paragraph refers to the final conflict without using specifics. We show that, somehow, Dantès escapes from prison with one thing on his mind: revenge. He's got the skills to get it done, but we make sure to include that dark side of his personality—the bitterness. Will it get in the way and possibly ruin everything? We can relate to where Dantès is after his unfair imprisonment. Such a universal struggle is easy for readers to relate to, so it's good to clarify that this is where the character is at the end without giving away his choice.

Word choice in the final paragraph is packed with action and emotion, reflecting the main character's state of mind as he goes about exacting his revenge. *Plunges* does double duty as a fine action word for how quickly

Dantès returns to civilization as well as for alluding to the actual method by which he escapes prison—but that's our secret. Readers who haven't read the book won't know that this is a giveaway, so it's acceptable to use. In addition, power words such as *arms, revenge, unjust, rage,* and *burns* fuel the sense of intensity. The final line contrasts *revenge on the guilty* with *spark tragic consequences for the innocent,* leaving open the question of Dantès's final choice.

Additionally, the text in the third paragraph could have easily read *he finds himself armed.* Generally, we try to avoid saying that any character finds himself or herself doing anything, because that implies they didn't mean to, which drops their competence a notch. In the end, the final word choice reflects Dantès's proactive intent, and instead of randomly discovering he has the tools he needs, he actively arms himself for his battle of revenge.

To be believable, heroes need flaws, but we should strive to include only the flaws we mean to show. We want the readers' focus to be on Dantès's struggle to control his bitter rage, not on his competence with the skills he learned in prison.

Whether you're writing a spy novel, a technothriller, a prison break, the capture of a terror cell, or any other sort of action/adventure story, it's the thrill of fast-paced action and up-to-the-challenge heroism that will draw readers to your novel. Promise it well with your description, and readers will trust that your book will deliver.

DON'T TRY THIS AT HOME

F INALLY, WE OFFER A SUMMARY of tactics and tricks to *avoid* using
when it's time to write up your description. For various reasons, these
are all very bad things, and they will all negatively affect your book's
first impression and, thus, your sales.

DON'T INCLUDE SUBPLOTS

Don't try to cram subplots into your book description. They'll overflow
your word limit, and readers will be likely to assume that the subplot has
equal importance with the main plot, which can lead to confusion and
disappointment. In addition, including subplots may dilute the awesomeness
of your main plot. After all, it's a subplot for a reason.

DON'T FALSELY ADVERTISE

Don't promise anything in your description that your story can't deliver. This
applies to everything, from tiny details you think would make your story
sound more appealing if you included them in the description all the way up
to entire secondary genre categories.

If you imply your book contains a plot element such as an intergalactic war,
it had better be a distinct element of your story and not a throwaway line of
dialogue somewhere. If you imply a secondary genre, such as romance, you
absolutely must have a good amount of distinct romance in your book. This
applies to all secondary genres you might include, but it especially applies to
romance. Never mess around with readers' expectation of romance. Don't
do it. That way lies one-star reviews.

DON'T DELAY THE READERS' IMMERSION

The very first words of your description should plunge your reader straight into the excitement of your story. Don't keep them outside the good stuff by starting with things like "This book is about…" or "This novel will make you…" Such phrases are unnecessary and distracting. They already know they're reading about a book, so you don't need to tell them that. If you have to tell them directly what your book is about, then your description isn't doing a good enough job of showing, and you should rewrite it.

Unless you can claim bestseller or award-winning status, leave your own name out of the book description. Don't use it to try to promote yourself separately from your book unless people will actually be so impressed that they'll automatically upgrade your book's potential before they even read it. The book description is exactly that: a description of your book. Not you. Feel free to add any awesome details about yourself in the author bio.

DON'T USE CLICHÉS

No matter how impressed you are with the guy who narrates movie trailers on TV, resist the urge to use the phrase *in a world where…* in your book description. Anywhere. Ever. Just no.

This goes for all other clichés you're tempted to use at any point, as well. If you're not sure whether you've used a cliché, think of how easily it came to mind. Did it pop into your mind as a whole phrase you've heard plenty of times before? Then it's probably a cliché.

Every book is unique. The words you use to describe these unique stories should also be crafted especially for them. Try to ensure that the only words you use to describe your novel are your own.

DON'T CHEAT WITH AN EXCERPT

If you have an epic line in your book that's also short enough to use for your tagline, go for it. But don't grab a few lines from your first chapter or a dramatic scene and use them for your entire book description. Books take thousands of words to explain the full heft of a plot. Cutting a tiny fragment from that tapestry will never do it justice like a properly crafted description will.

Don't get facty

Some genres are more prone to this issue than others, especially those that have to explain worldbuilding details. But every book has the potential to fall into the trap of telling—separating the facts of the story from the action—instead of showing. Here's a facty description to consider:

"It's 1303. The place is Verona, Italy. In this day and age, family rivalries are strong. Two powerful houses known as the Montagues and Capulets are upholding their traditional grudges against each other, but their children are about to fall in love. Watch as Romeo and Juliet feel all the feels. They know their families will never approve, but they can't help themselves. Teenagers these days."

See all the telling? The year, the location, the overexplaining about the rivalries, the lovers' actions. None of that needs to be spelled out for readers. Context, if written properly, will give readers everything they need to know.

"Medieval Italy is no place for fifteen-year-old Juliet to fall in love with the son of her father's bitterest rival."

You totally just thought of medieval torture devices, didn't you? We did, and we already know this storyline. One good sentence of showing will always outshine a whole paragraph of telling, giving you more reader draw for your word count.

Don't use negative trigger concepts or words

Word choice is always important when you have only two hundred words to make readers fall in love with your story. However, sometimes it's not about making a positive impression so much as avoiding making a negative one. Clarity and intent can make all the difference between describing an imminent bestseller and describing something that sinks your sales with an unintended negative implication.

When your description is complete, read back through it and see if any of the words trigger a negative association. Think of words like *childish* instead of *innocent* or *childlike*. Or perhaps you have a phrase like *after she quit school*, which may make your character seem to possess the negative stereotypical traits readers assign to high school dropouts. Rewording to express the same event in a more positive light can make readers view your character more sympathetically: *after she was forced to give up her dreams of college* paints the same character and same situation in a different and more positive light.

It's highly advisable to have at least one other person read through your description, as well. This second set of eyes may see negative implications that you don't. And definitely set the description aside for a day or more before looking at it one last time. The less you remember about all that hard work picking and choosing words, the fresher their impact will strike you when you reread, and the more objective your view will be.

This level of perusal is pretty intense, requiring you to look at every word and every phrase you've put into your description and analyze it for what it may mean to readers in your target audience. But it's a critical step to ensuring that you have said everything you mean to say—and nothing you didn't.

DON'T ASSUME YOU DON'T NEED A DESCRIPTION AT ALL

You do. The first thing a potential reader will see when shopping online is a thumbnail of the book cover. Cover art is critical to enticing the reader to click through to the book page. Once they're there, the next thing they're going to do is read your book description. These are your two chances to literally sell your book. If you don't complete one of these steps, you're cutting your success rate in half.

The job of your cover art is to provide visual symbols for the book's content and tone. It is in no way a substitute for a good book description. Descriptive text specifies how the symbolism of the cover art plays out in plot and character. If you don't delineate in black and white exactly how awesome your book is going to be, readers won't want to buy it based on imagery alone.

DON'T LEAD OFF YOUR BOOK DESCRIPTION SECTION WITH EDITORIAL REVIEWS

Conceptually related to the reason you don't want your book description to be too long in word count or paragraph number, this guideline is based on the principle that it's rude to make your potential readers click the Show More link. Don't write so much, in any regard, that they have to expand the field in order to figure out what you're telling them. Keep it short, keep it on topic, and keep it awesome.

ABOUT THE AUTHOR

Kris James is Executive Marketing Director at Red Adept Publishing. She holds a BA in English Literature from Pacific Union College.

Her published fiction writing, under such pen names as Morgan C. Talbot and Jasmine Giacomo, covers four genres and includes nine full-length novels. Her short stories have been published in magazines, ezines, audio format, and anthologies. She lives in Washington.

BEYOND the STYLE MANUAL

Red Adept Publishing

GET TO the POINT
TRIMMING UNNECESSARY WORDS

INTRODUCTION

It's true—sometimes, less is more. A lot of clunky extras can weigh down—and even bury—the well-written parts that should be the focal point of your writing. A short, terrific piece that tells your story can be better than a long, bloated "masterpiece" no one will ever be brave enough to tackle. Your words should serve your intention: for people to read and think about your message. The words themselves are important, but the ideas behind the words are why readers pick up a book. When the writing doesn't deliver the message, it isn't doing its job. And when your writing isn't doing its job, it needs to be trimmed.

Drawing in a reader is one thing, but keeping a reader is another. The best writers understand how to hold a reader's attention. Convoluted, wordy writing draws focus away from the content and makes readers work harder than necessary. This guide discusses how to streamline your writing into more efficient and effective prose. I'll explain how to find and eliminate wordiness and redundancy so that you can avoid unnecessary explanations and excessive descriptions. Then you can work on making your long, clunky sentences into more concise, cleaner prose. And the quiz at the end of the book will even give you a little practice.

Ladies and gentlemen, let's get to the point!

CHAPTER 1:
REDUCING REDUNDANCY AND WORDINESS

Wording can easily run off with the meaning, especially during an intense writing session when you're trying to get your thoughts down. In the heat of the moment, all you could think of was *running slowly*. But when you came back to the passage after letting it sit for a while, you realized that *jogging* was better.

Crazy wording can be tough to avoid during the creative process, but wordiness can be easier to catch on a reread, and it's a big part of the weedy stuff that can clutter up your writing. But good writing should be a manicured lawn. And the trouble with the wordy bits isn't just that they're bogging down your writing; they might even be obscuring your meaning. Consider this bit of wordy writing:

> Crouching down, I gripped the hilt of my sword with my fingers, aware of my legs being bent at the middle, ready to spring. Then I pulled my sword from the protective case holding it at my hip. I pushed up with my legs, moving my arm quickly and sharply cutting the air.

This passage is really wordy, and it's the kind of thing that makes total sense to a writer in the heat of the moment, and probably even when he rereads without taking careful stock. But to a reader, it can be confusing. What exactly is happening with the legs? And where is that sword? Take a look at the cleaned-up version:

> Crouching, I gripped the hilt of my sword, aware of the tension in my knees. I drew my sword from the scabbard at my hip. Then I sprang, swinging my arm and slicing the air.

This version makes more sense than the original did. Some of the issues with the original passage are just wordiness. For example, the word *tension* steps in for *ready to spring*, and the definition of *scabbard* already includes the information that it protects the blade of the sword. You'll usually find that choosing better substitutes for clunky writing is easier once you've let your brain settle down.

Using more words than is necessary to relay an idea results in pleonasm, which is fancy editorspeak for being redundant. Really, most of this book is about pleonasm, but this section focuses on the small wording issues rather than the repetition of big ideas. Repetition can be used stylistically to emphasize an idea, but you might be doubling up on wording without even realizing it because plenty of redundant phrases slip into everyday speech. Don't tolerate them sneaking in and weighing down your writing.

Sometimes, even basic descriptions can get wordy, no matter how short they are. Instead of describing a character as having or being something, using an adjective often works better.

> **Clunky:** The man had green eyes, and he turned his sinister gaze on me.

> **Cleaner:** The green-eyed man turned his sinister gaze on me.

> **Clunky:** Her eyes were blue and full of fire.

> **Cleaner:** Her blue eyes were full of fire.

Beware repetitive adjectives, as well. Nearly every word has synonyms. Adjectives with the same meaning often pile up on unsuspecting authors and create redundancies.

> **Clunky:** The terrified and frightened children scattered when they saw the monster.

Cleaner: The terrified children scattered when they saw the monster.

Clunky: The bright, radiant sun shined on the lake.

Cleaner: The radiant sun shined on the lake.

Clunky: The winter had been long, and the deer were hungry and starving.

Cleaner: The winter had been long, and the deer were starving.

Consider these passages where the first sentence says pretty much the same as the second:

Clunky: The drug's effect was instantly palpable. He could feel it immediately.

Cleaner: The drug's effect was instantly palpable.

Explanation: *Palpable* means capable of being felt, and *immediately* is the same as *instantly.*

Clunky: Suzanne had faith in his plan. She knew it would work.

Cleaner: Suzanne had faith his plan would work.

Explanation: *Having faith in* and *knowing that something would work* express the same idea.

Clunky: He worked at the puzzle, trying everything he could think of until he'd exhausted all of his ideas.

Cleaner: He worked at the puzzle, exhausting all of his ideas.

Explanation: *Trying everything he could think of* means that he *exhausted all of his ideas.*

Among the most common redundancies editors see are words used in conjunction with other words or phrases that describe ideas already included in the definition of one of the other words involved. *Nodding* and *shrugging* are great examples. *Nodding* by definition involves motion of the head, so you never need to say that a character *nods his head. Shrugging* includes the motion of the shoulders in its definition, so you never need to say that a character *shrugs his shoulders.* Lots of actions involving body parts are easy to overdescribe. Keep in mind that kicking always uses the feet or legs, punching always involves a fist, and blinking is always done with the eyes.

But redundant wording goes beyond the motions of body parts. Here is a list of common pleonasms to avoid:

- absolutely necessary

- advanced preview

- advanced warning

- ascend up

- blinking with the eyes

- circled around

- completely and utterly

- connect together

- constant nagging

- descend down

- exact same

- exhale out

- fall down

- final solution

- follow behind

- free gift

- frozen solid

- ice cold

- inhale in

- kick with a foot

- known suspect

- nod with the head

- pair of twins

- past experience

- point with a finger

- punch with a fist

- retreated back

- scatter this way and that

- shatter into pieces

- shrug with the shoulders

- sink down

- splinter into pieces

- step on with a foot

- stumble awkwardly

- temporary (or momentary) reprieve

- topple over

- tumble and fall

- unexpected surprise

- unmarried bachelor

- wave with a hand

- zigzag back and forth

Common sense can often help you recognize a redundancy. Some redundancies can be sorted out by asking, "Could there be any other kind?" and "Is there already a word for that?" Take *punching* as an example. If a character punches someone with his fist, that's redundant because "to punch" *means* to hit with the fist. Even if we didn't know that the definition of *punch* includes using a fist, you can still ask yourself, "Could I punch someone with anything other than my fist?" You could hit someone with an open hand, but that's called a slap. You could hit someone with your elbow, but that would be elbowing. Ways of hitting that are similar to punching but use a body part other than the fist already have words to describe them. And think of *to stumble awkwardly*. There's really no graceful way to stumble, so the awkwardness is implied.

However, sometimes seemingly redundant wording is necessary in order to include pertinent additional information. If that's the case, be sure to follow through on the idea. For example, if you mention that a character punched with his fist for a specific reason, make sure you include the significance of that reason. Maybe you mean to tell the reader that a character didn't do much damage because he hit someone with a *loose* fist. Or maybe you mean to tell the reader that he used a really *tight* fist, which is why he broke his finger. The following sentences also involve redundancies that have a purpose:

Example: The room was really clean. In fact, it was spotless. Anna had obviously been very busy.

Explanation: The repetition demonstrates that the narrator noticed the room is clean then takes a closer look and realizes just how much work Anna has done.

Example: Patrick looked thin—gaunt even. Jessica wondered how long he'd gone without eating.

Explanation: The repetition of the idea of thin with *gaunt* represents emphasis rather than tautology, which is needlessly saying the same thing twice but with different words. The emphasis in this example reinforces the idea that Patrick is thin enough that Jessica has a legitimate reason to be concerned.

Example: When I saw the mess they'd made, I couldn't believe my eyes. I just couldn't comprehend the disaster they had created in my living room.

Explanation: Here, the narrator is struggling to come to terms with a massive mess, which he's probably going to have to clean up himself, so he's repeated it to emphasize the effort he's putting into that comprehension.

If you're going to use repetition, make sure it has a purpose. But using repetition too often can weaken the tool. So use it sparingly and only when you're certain it works, or it's going to seem accidental, which is no good.

But some kinds of redundancies never have a purpose. Adverbs that create pairs and build lists are very useful, but doubling up on them is never okay. Pay attention to words and phrases like these:

- additionally

- also

- as well

- as well as

- besides

- in addition to

- likewise

- too

These words all signal that the nouns before, after, or around them are components in a set or part of a list. Careful writers avoid doubling up on these adverbs because doing so can confuse which people, things, or ideas are definitely involved in the set. Using more of these words in a sentence than is necessary is a common mistake. Look out for sentences like these:

Clunky: In addition to the chicken, John ordered the lobster, as well.

Cleaner: In addition to the chicken, John ordered the lobster.

Clunky: Besides the expensive car, he'd made other questionable financial decisions, too.

Cleaner: Besides the expensive car, he'd made other questionable financial decisions.

Clunky: He went to the store and the bank also.

Cleaner: He went to the store and the bank.

Additionally, keep an eye out for acronyms (abbreviations derived from the first letters of each word in a phrase or term) that already include words that are often tacked on after the acronym. This kind of repetition is another example of redundancy that serves no purpose. For example, ATM is short for *automated teller machine*. This acronym already includes the word *machine*, so it is redundant to say *ATM machine* because you're actually repeating *machine*. It's like saying *automated teller machine machine*. The same goes for PIN, which is an acronym for *personal identification number*. People often say things like, "I need your PIN number." However, that's technically redundant because they're actually saying *number* twice. Even Latin words and words derived from foreign languages get in on the action. *Et cetera* means "and so forth." So, even when it is abbreviated to *etc.*, the word *and* should never precede it. That would mean using *and* twice. Because they slip into everyday speech, these types of redundancies could work well to make dialogue seem more natural, but keep them out of the rest of your writing.

Avoid these common redundancies with acronyms:

- ABS system (antilock braking system system)

- ATM machine (automated teller machine machine)

- HIV virus (*human immunodeficiency virus virus)*

- ISBN number (International Standard Book Number number)

- PC computer (personal computer computer)

- PIN number (personal identification number number)

Times of day also have special abbreviations that you should be careful not to make redundant. From midnight to noon is always a.m., and noon to midnight is always p.m. The following examples include redundant phrasing involving the time of day:

Clunky: Our morning meeting was early—at five o'clock a.m.

Cleaner: Our morning meeting was early—five o'clock!

Clunky: The afternoon train leaves at 3:00 p.m. sharp.

Cleaner: The afternoon train leaves at 3:00 sharp.

And to avoid redundancy—or confusion—over 12:00 p.m. and 12:00 a.m., just use *noon* and *midnight*. In fact, many style manuals prefer *noon* and *midnight* to *twelve o'clock*.

Redundancy can still linger even when you've cleaned up around special terms, and entire ideas might get dragged into the fray. A few redundant phrases often accompany specific ideas, and they are easy to avoid once you recognize them. So please remember:

- A trap is by definition created to prevent escape, so you never need to say anything is caught in a trap with no escape.

- Murder must obviously involve death, or it isn't murder, so *murdered to death* is redundant.

- The leader is always ahead, and the follower is always behind. Describing someone as *following behind* is unnecessary.

- Returning is always coming back again, so if someone *returns again*, they have been there *three* times, not just two.

- A lie is always false or untrue. Characters need not claim that lies are false if they've already called the statement a lie.

- Suddenly is always without warning and usually unexpected. Avoid calling surprises sudden and unexpected.

- The word *imminent* always describes things that are about to happen. You'll never need to describe things that are imminent as happening soon.

And consider phrases like *fairly unique*. The concept of uniqueness is singular—it doesn't have phases or exist on a spectrum. To be unique is to be one of a kind. That means there are no others like it. So the word *unique* never takes a modifier. Nothing will ever be *pretty unique*, *completely unique*, or *somewhat unique*. If you feel the need to attach an adverb to *unique*, then you probably mean *rare* or *unusual*, which have meanings similar to *unique* but without suggesting that the item in question is one of a kind.

Many words have definitions that already include the idea of being complete. So these words cannot be described as being *more than* or *completely* without being illogical or redundant. Take, for example, *full*. A glass that is *totally full* is simply *full*. If you're trying to say that it is more than full, then you need something like *overflowing* to get that job done. Or consider *perfect*: nothing *less than perfect* is actually *perfect*. And there's nothing *more perfect* than *perfect*. So *perfect* is simply *perfect*. Keep an eye out for similar redundancies like these:

- completely empty

- completely gone

- completely transparent

- entirely soaked/soaked through

- more/less perfect

- thoroughly exhausted

- totally disappeared

Several of the examples above might sound like figures of speech. Some editors will let common figures of speech slide even if they're redundant, but other editors, and careful readers, might not be so accepting. So keep in mind that these figures of speech are actually redundant:

- above and beyond

- cease and desist

- conniption fit

- each and every

- for all intents and purposes

Though many of the examples of redundant wording in this section have gained purchase in everyday speech, they don't belong in writing. Be mindful of the definitions of the words you're using, and choose carefully to avoid redundancy. Cutting isn't *always* the solution to a redundancy. And sometimes, redundancy isn't redundant at all. But writers who include accidental redundancies run the risk of losing the emphasis on the repetition that does have meaning behind it. Taking careful stock of your writing helps tame the wild weeds that choke out the truly great stuff you've written.

CHAPTER 2:
COMMON CLUNKERS

Redundancy isn't the only problem that can lead to unwieldy writing. Some words simply create clunky sentence structures. A few of the most common clunkers slip into everyday speech—and, therefore, into writing—but careful writers avoid them because they don't provide necessary information or sound particularly eloquent.

Take a close look at sentences that include phrases like *it was* and *there was*. If the pronouns *it* and *there* aren't replacing actual nouns, then you might not need them. To trim them, just give the word order a little flip so the subject takes the initial position.

Clunky: There was nothing he could do to help.

Cleaner: He could do nothing to help.

Clunky: It was the principle of the idea at issue.

Cleaner: The principle of the idea was at issue.

In the cases below, *there were* and *there wasn't* are even paired up with other extra words (e.g., *that* and *that were*) in an attempt to smooth out the clunker.

Clunky: There were a million things that he had on his mind.

Cleaner: He had a million things on his mind.

Clunky: There were tons of ideas that were floating around the boardroom.

Cleaner: Tons of ideas floated around the boardroom.

Clunky: There wasn't any way cleaning up the mess could have been avoided.

Cleaner: Cleaning up the mess couldn't have been avoided.

Sometimes you'll get a clunker that needs more than a word-order flip. It might need a massage to work out the kinks around those phrases like *it was* and *there was*. And gerunds are fabulous masseurs. A gerund is a present-participle verb that functions as a noun, so it can perform actions just as a noun could. In the examples below, a gerund helps clear up the clutter.

Clunky: It was his idea to sell the house.

Cleaner: Selling the house was his idea.

(*Selling* the house is the gerund.)

Clunky: It was John's responsibility to clean the room.

Cleaner: Cleaning the room was John's responsibility.

(*Cleaning* the room is the gerund.)

Sometimes cutting the clunker doesn't make the sentence shorter, but it can make your wording more interesting, or at least more direct.

Clunky: It was his only choice.

Cleaner: He had no other choice.

Clunky: It was just before daylight the next day when the men ventured out.

Cleaner: Just before daylight the next day, the men ventured out.

Passive voice isn't actually a grammar error, but it is often considered weak writing and can clutter up your sentences. When the object of an action functions as the subject of the sentence, passive voice has crept into your writing. And this can often make the intention or the action itself unclear. Then the words get all twisted up and start dragging other, unnecessary words into the sentence.

Clunky (passive voice): The coffin was carried by the pallbearers.

Cleaner (active voice): The pallbearers carried the coffin.

In the clunker, the pallbearers are the ones doing the action, but they aren't in the spot in the sentence where readers usually expect to see the grammatical subject. And we had to toss in extra words just to make that whole thing work. Here's another example:

Clunky (passive voice): The hedges were trimmed by the gardener.

Cleaner (active voice): The gardener trimmed the hedges.

Passive voice can make sentences even more awkward when it discards the important information entirely. So pay close attention to sentences that look like the following example:

Clunky (passive voice): The man was hit in the head by the rock.

Clunky (passive voice with missing information): The man was hit in the head.

Cleaner (active voice): The big rock hit the man in the head.

In the active voice, you can see what was missing from that passive-voice sentence: the rock.

In active or passive voice, extraneous prepositions or prepositional phrases can bloat sentences, too. A preposition links nouns, pronouns, gerunds, and noun phrases to other words in a sentence, and phrases that start with prepositions are called prepositional phrases. The English language uses many prepositions, but here's a list of common ones:

- about
- around
- at
- before
- in
- into
- of
- on
- onto
- through
- toward
- upon

Sometimes, writers get carried away with prepositions. After all, they're pretty handy. But relying too heavily on prepositions can make your writing cumbersome. So be on the lookout for unnecessary prepositions and prepositional phrases.

Clunky: The spear pierced through the knight's armor.

Cleaner: The spear pierced the knight's armor.

Above, the clunker includes an extra preposition whose idea is carried in the definition of the verb it's paired with. The word *pierced* means "to go through" or "to make a hole through." So the definition of *pierced* covers the idea that the object doing the piercing went *through* whatever it pierced. The preposition *through* is, therefore, unnecessary. In the examples below, you'll see useful prepositions that are tangled up with extraneous prepositions. Each of these sentences does need one preposition, but none of them need two:

Clunky: The bat flew away toward the window.

Cleaner: The bat flew toward the window.

Clunky: Larry finally coaxed the frightened dog out from under the table.

Cleaner: Larry finally coaxed the frightened dog from under the table.

Other times, the solutions to preposition troubles aren't as cut and dried as choosing which one to keep. A single preposition might have the same meaning as a clunky pair of prepositions.

Clunky: He went to stand over by the lamp.

Cleaner: He went to stand near the lamp.

Clunky: I laid the picnic blanket right over the top of an ant hill.

Cleaner: I laid the picnic blanket right on an ant hill.

Sometimes sentences need only a single preposition because the stuff going on in the prepositional phrase is implied. In nearly all contexts, the reader can reasonably assume certain things about the world to be true. This means they can make connections without needing the connections explained, and those unneeded explanations often turn up in the form of extra prepositional phrases; for example:

Clunky: I packed my lunch into my lunchbox.

Cleaner: I packed my lunchbox.

In the above example, the author can reasonably expect the reader to assume that lunch is going in the lunchbox. If the character's circumstances mean that he might be packing something strange in that lunchbox—you know, severed hands or stolen diamonds—then, by all means, keep the extra distinction. But if you're talking humdrum packing-lunch-in-the-morning stuff, then there's no need to specify. Consider this example:

> **Clunky:** Standing in the center of the rug, Lisa turned slowly, surveying the room around her.

> **Cleaner:** Standing in the center of the rug, Lisa turned slowly, surveying the room.

Lisa is obviously looking at the things in the room around her. Her action and her placement on the rug tell the reader that she is looking at the room where she is standing, so *around her* is extraneous. If she had been looking at a security camera or something of that nature, the specification might have been necessary.

Here's another handy tip to trim prepositions: the word *of* should never follow *off*. You can—and should—always trim the *of* because it is implied by the *off.*

> **Clunky:** I stepped off of the curb.

> **Cleaner:** I stepped off the curb.

> **Clunky:** The sailor fell off of the boat.

> **Cleaner:** The sailor fell off the boat.

Common clunkers require special attention because they can seem correct. They sound right to the ear because we hear them so often in everyday speech. And remember, they are perfectly acceptable in dialogue because people really do speak that way. Using common clunkers and mistakes that people make when speaking makes dialogues flow more naturally, and it lends realism to the characters' voices. However, when used in narration, they are more likely to clutter up your pages.

CHAPTER 3:
DUCKING THE DIRECT DESCRIPTION

Quite often, authors just can't seem to commit to the wording they have chosen. A description starts out strong then falters when the author includes an adverb that diminishes the meaning of the description. Don't hedge on descriptions by pulling away from a great metaphor or a sturdy adjective by adding too many adverbs. Just go for it; make the commitment. Whenever you find yourself adding extra adverbs, take a step back—even if you have to drag yourself away—and consider if there's another, more precise word that means just what you were trying to get at by adding the adverb. You might need a new adjective instead of an adverb. Be on the lookout for these descriptive words that are likely to steal the thunder from your adjective or that are simply weaker than another, stronger adjective might be:

- almost

- kind of

- nearly

- pretty much

- sort of

- some kind of

- some sort of

- somewhat

The following examples illustrate these issues:

Clunky: He was pretty mad.

Cleaner: He was livid.

Clunky: The house was kind of big.

Cleaner: The house was enormous.

Clunky: John got punched a lot.

Cleaner: John got pummeled.

Clunky: The family was very poor.

Cleaner: The family was destitute.

Clunky: She flashed him a super bright smile.

Cleaner: She flashed him a dazzling smile.

Clunky: I hid the note in a hard-to-notice spot.

Cleaner: I hid the note in an inconspicuous spot.

Some descriptions, however, are purposely vague, and numbers and measurements can be especially tricky. You don't want to have the narrator seemingly running around with a tape measure in order to dole out exact measurements of everything. And unless the narrator has exceptional counting skills, he's not going to be able to count everything, either. So you'll need to make estimates, which are a necessary form of hedging. However, that doesn't mean you should run wild with the extra adverbs. When estimates involve certain words or phrases—like *give or take*, *around*, or *more than*—you won't need *almost*, *nearly*, and the like. If you're already estimating, you have no reason to estimate that estimate. Check out the examples below:

Clunky: The wall was about chest high.

Cleaner: The wall was chest high.

Not everyone's chest is the same height, but *chest high* is clearly an estimate from the narrator's point of view. And in an entire book, there's plenty of room elsewhere to tell the readers whether this narrator is tall or short, so readers can take it from there. If the wall was meant to be slightly lower than chest high, you could just say *waist high*. If it was taller than chest high, then you could use *neck high* or *head high*. So there's no need for *about*. The idea that this is an inexact measurement is implied by the description itself.

Here are examples of another estimation issue that slips into all kinds of writing:

Clunky: The store has a whole bunch of books, maybe even more than a thousand.

Cleaner: The store has more than a thousand books.

More than a thousand is already an estimate that includes the idea of being more than one hundred. *Maybe even more* at the end doubled up on the idea of surpassing one hundred. Additionally, avoid this kind of thing:

Clunky: The store has over one hundred to two hundred books in stock.

Cleaner: The store has over one hundred books in stock.

The clunker above doesn't really make logical sense. Does this store have more than one hundred books or more than two hundred books? Two hundred must be more than one hundred, so if this store has two hundred books, then having more than one hundred is obvious. And this store might actually have more than two hundred books in stock, which would simply be *hundreds* or *over two hundred*. Maybe this store actually has *between* one hundred and two hundred books. Numbers are easy to bobble if you don't stop to think about them carefully. And when hedging creates redundant numbers, that can put your count way off, shooting your estimate out of the ballpark and into outer space.

As with measurements and counts, there will be other times when you legitimately need something less than decisive. So save the hedging for moments when things didn't happen but almost did—and when the difference is important. Making sure to keep the accidental hedging out of your writing lends legitimacy to the times when you do pull back from the straightforward description:

>**Example:** His kiss nearly swept her off her feet.

>**Explanation:** If he didn't sweep her off her feet, she might still be looking for the gent who can. She might not have felt the spark she was expecting. There's meaning behind missing the mark on this one. If it was a fantastic kiss, it should have simply swept her off her feet.

>**Example:** Alice was almost angry enough to murder someone.

>**Explanation:** The difference between *almost* murdering someone and actually murdering someone is a huge one. If she is mad enough to kill someone, she'll probably be hiding murder weapons or hiring lawyers.

>**Example:** Sharon hated her job so much that she was nearly ready to quit.

>**Explanation:** Sharon didn't quit—she has a lot of bills to pay—so *nearly* serves to tell the reader how aggravated Sharon is, even though she can't afford to quit.

So there are times that you can hedge on the descriptions, and there are even times when you'll *need* to, but most of the time, you'll want to avoid it. Be judicious with your use of adverbs and be open to new, more precise adjectives that avoid wordiness.

CHAPTER 4:
WORDY METAPHORS AND SIMILES

Wordy bits can sneak in around descriptions where the writer tries to create something eloquent but turns it clunky instead. Figurative language is often the culprit in these situations. Similes and metaphors, two kinds of figurative language, are lovely little tools for description, but they can go awry. A simile is a phrase that uses the word *like* or *as* to describe something by comparing it to another thing with one or several similar qualities. A metaphor is a figure of speech in which a word or phrase actually replaces another in order to draw an analogy. Here are a few examples:

Simile: He looked like a wild animal prowling the night.

Metaphor: He was a wild animal prowling the night.

Simile: The bird let out a shriek like a banshee, and the sound startled us.

Metaphor: The bird's banshee shriek startled us.

Simile: The tow-truck driver was like her knight in shining armor.

Metaphor: The tow-truck driver was her knight in shining armor.

Metaphors can draw fantastic visuals without being as wordy as similes. And when you use a metaphor, it's better to just dive straight in for the metaphor rather than getting really wordy in an attempt to explain to the reader that you've used a metaphor. If you have to explain what you're doing with your writing, you might have gone about it from the wrong direction.

Instead of saying, "He made Heather feel as if a fire had been lit in her heart," just commit to the image and say, "He lit a fire in Heather's heart." Unless you're writing a sci-fi novel in which technology makes it possible to light people's insides on fire or you have a firestarter running amok, the reader is probably sharp enough to understand that the phrase refers to inspiring romantic feelings and is not meant to be taken literally. Of course, there are always contexts where the metaphor might be mistaken for something that could really happen. Science fiction and fantasy stories are probably the most likely to require serious attention when you're looking to use metaphors instead of similes. When you have a sci-fi character who can actually kill people by looking at them, the phrase *if looks could kill* takes on a very literal meaning. So you'll need to avoid this character's eyes burning holes in people when they stare intensely and the like, because he literally could do so.

Because similes use the preposition *like*, understanding the usage of the word is important to crafting proper similes. Traditionally, the preposition *like* is used as an adjective, rather than an adverb, and it is followed by a noun or pronoun that functions as an object of the sentence, phrase, or clause. Think of it as comparing a thing to a thing, whereas *as if* and *as though* compare how that thing acts or behaves to how another thing acts or behaves. Here's an example:

> **Clunky:** The woman's expression made her look as though she were a mouse.

> **Cleaner:** The woman looked like a mouse.

In the case of this woman who looks like a mouse, the author need not use *as though* to compare how she looks to how a mouse looks when comparing the woman directly to the mouse would mean the same thing.

Here's another example where the metaphor is going to be obvious *nearly* every time:

Clunky: He felt cold, as if ice were running in his veins.

Cleaner: He had ice in his veins.

Ice is obviously cold, and blood is obviously in veins. Unless you've placed the character in a situation or world where his blood might freeze without killing him, the reader will understand that he doesn't really have ice or cold blood in his veins. He would be dead if that were the case. So if the character is still moving around and having conversations, he's obviously not dead—or frozen.

So don't pull back from your descriptions when you've drawn a sharp correlation. That usually just ruins something cool. Metaphors are fantastic writing tools, while similes frequently make sentences clunky and heavy. Often, a metaphor would have sounded better and maintained the idea just as well as a simile could have. Consider the following example:

Simile: Jack's disguise made him look like an old, portly man instead of the young, thin man he was.

Metaphor: Jack's disguise transformed him from a young, thin man into an old, portly man.

Then there are times when a comparison is needed, but a simile is not necessary to make that comparison. Sometimes a comparison is useful and appropriate, but the description doesn't require a metaphor or a simile because the thing being described is actually the same as the thing that it is being compared to. It isn't *like* the other thing; it *is* the other thing. Consider this example:

Clunky: Anna looked like an attractive woman.

Cleaner: Anna looked attractive.

For this example, I'll establish a little background. Let's say Anna is definitely a woman. Anna has taken a little extra effort with her appearance in this scene, and the narrator has failed to take notice of Anna's attractiveness before. Still, Anna doesn't look *like* an attractive woman—she *is* an attractive woman—the narrator just hasn't noticed until now. So the simile simply isn't necessary.

Now, you don't need to avoid similes like the plague. They're a perfectly acceptable tool for your writer's toolbox, but don't lean on them like a crutch and let your metaphor-writing muscles atrophy.

CHAPTER 5:
SHOW AND TELL

On occasion, wordiness infects entire passages. Be careful of whole scenes that run away with the show. For instance, it can be tempting to use inside jokes in the narrative, but since the meanings of inside jokes are by nature shared by only a few, lots of explanation would be required to get the idea across. But at a certain point, the explanation eats up so much narrative that readers lose track of what's going on. Or even worse, they get bored while slogging through the setup for the joke. If they continually get bored or confused, readers are likely to give up on your book. Sure, your friends and family will think it's hilarious, but aren't you hoping your audience will be broader than that?

If you create worlds and characters that draw the reader into the story, the things that happen along the way become the inside jokes and experiences that your reader shares with the characters. Bring the reader along on the adventure that sets up the joke or shared experience rather than forcing the information or backstory into the book.

Sometimes an "info dump" can masquerade as important information. Even when the information is useful, resist the urge to dump a bunch of background into the narration or dialogue. Doing so can stop the forward momentum of the story. If it's pertinent to the story, the information should flow smoothly with the narrative and dialogue. It might need to be sprinkled in along the way. For example, if you're writing a murder mystery and you've given a character a PhD in entomology, there's no reason to explain in detail how he knows what he knows about insects. You might describe the processes he uses to come to his conclusions, but there's no need to cite specific studies on fruit flies that this character studied while at university. He obviously studied lots and lots of research before graduating with a PhD. If the information is necessary, it should be interwoven with the narrative or dialogue. Don't give up too much all at once. And if it's not necessary information, it probably shouldn't be there at all. Avoid stopping the plot to drop interesting but irrelevant information into your book.

The same goes for superfluous dialogue. Are your characters having discussions just for the sake of having discussions? Is the dialogue you're showing the reader important to the story? Are they talking on and on about a party they went to weeks ago? Too much small talk isn't a good idea. A teeny bit can make an exchange feel natural, but if it doesn't involve what's going on with the plot we're in now, maybe readers don't need to hear about it. Friends obviously share special moments; you don't need to beat the readers over the head with that idea by making them read paragraphs of dialogue that prove what they already assumed. Stick to dialogue that applies to what's going on in the story or shows character development.

Scenes with dialogue that doesn't push the story forward are not your friend. If a serial killer is chasing your two female leads, the girls probably shouldn't stop to gossip about boys. That doesn't serve the plot, and it won't feel natural because they should be more worried about not getting killed than getting asked out on a second date.

Don't spend a bunch of time telling readers backstory about a relationship unless it matters at that point. Keep the characters on task with their dialogue and always consider their emotions at the moment. Don't have them stop to talk about things that they wouldn't be worried about right then. Maintain proper tension.

Too much simple back-and-forth can also eat up space—and a reader's patience. Avoid having characters repeat dialogue that another character just said or having a character ask another to repeat things. That might go something like this:

> "Did I tell you that I bought that leather jacket we saw in the store on Friday?" Sue asked.
> "No," Jill said.

"Well, I did."

"Oh, cool," Jill said, sounding annoyed.

For the sake of the above example, assume the jacket is important to the story. The author needs the reader to know that Sue bought the jacket and that Jill now knows that Sue bought the jacket. So this clunker could be tightened into:

"Hey, I bought that leather jacket we saw in the store on Friday," Sue said.

"Oh, cool," Jill said, sounding annoyed.

The following example is simply too repetitive:

"Did you take the freeway?" Jill asked.

"Yeah, I took the freeway," Sue said.

"Why did you take the freeway?"

"I took the freeway because I thought it would be quicker."

Dumping the repetitive dialogue doesn't necessarily mean discarding the conversation. The speakers may just be repeating words back and forth without adding new information to the dialogue. That clunker can be cleaned up like this:

"Did you take the freeway?" Jill asked.

"Yeah," Sue said.

"Why?"

"I thought it would be quicker."

Some writers use dialogue as a tool to present backstory or to explain complicated things. And that is a perfectly acceptable way to get this information to the reader. When done with finesse, this technique can enhance the flow of the story and avoid info dumps. However, especially in science fiction or fantasy novels, authors sometimes use a dialogue exchange to explain complicated ideas. One character explains the inner workings of a machine or the principles behind a magical occurrence, and the explanation is too complicated for the second character to understand. During the ensuing conversation, the second character asks lots of questions, and the first character must explain the idea several times, each time bringing it closer to the listener's level of understanding. This is no doubt because the author worries that the reader won't understand the first description. Whenever the explanation—and this advice applies to explanations even if they show up outside dialogue—is complicated enough that you feel the need to explain a second time with simpler wording or by using a comparison to something more common, just start out with that easier explanation. Rather than presenting two explanations, use the easier one first.

Like superfluous dialogue, peripheral characters can take up too much of readers' time (and can confuse them about what's really important in the story). Don't spend a lot of time describing and giving names to characters who show up for only a second. Not every character needs a name. Even if the narrator knows the person's name, it's not necessarily worth going into a bunch of detail over. Consider this line:

> I spotted Mary Drummond, a girl from my third-period chemistry class, but I wasn't in the mood to talk, so I pretended not to see her when she waved from across the mall.

In this case, Mary exists only to shed light on our narrator's bad mood. Mary isn't going to show up again. Neither is the chemistry class. So there's no real reason for all that information. This part isn't about Mary at all. It could have been anyone, and our narrator wouldn't have wanted to talk. A fix might look like this:

> I spotted a girl from school, but I wasn't in the mood to talk to anyone, so I pretended not to see her when she waved from across the mall.

You might even have characters who don't need to be there at all. If you stop to describe the creepy guy in the drugstore, he had better try to rob the joint or follow one of your characters home. Or maybe the lead character wonders if this man is his long-lost father, or the main character might be hungover from the night before and wondering if he looks like this creepy guy. Creepy Dude needs to be important to the story somehow or representative of how the character is feeling. Otherwise, he's just one of the creepy dudes roaming the streets, and we all see those guys, so that's like telling the readers that there's a refrigerator in the kitchen. We all know they're there, and if they aren't important to the story, you don't need to mention them. The mundane things about life are part of almost every reader's experience. If you simply put the characters in the situations, the regular bits fill themselves in. Your job is to point out the important or unusual elements of the characters' world.

Remember, however, that there are times when peripheral characters do serve a purpose and, therefore, warrant a detailed description. Perhaps the narrator is feeling self-conscious and wonders if he's looking a lot like Creepy Dude. Then Creepy Dude's description is important because it tells us something about how the narrator is feeling. Just be sure you clarify the correlation between what he's seeing and what he's feeling. Or perhaps while the narrator is hung up worrying that the overtly strange-looking fellow is up to something fishy, the narrator fails to notice when the guy in the business suit pulls a gun. In that case, Creepy Dude pushes the plot forward. Avoid overdescribing mundane things just because they exist for the character. The aspects that set them apart are important. That's what makes for good storytelling.

Being aware of "show" and "tell" also helps you delve deeper into good storytelling. Once you've shown the readers something, you don't necessarily need to *tell* them about it, as well. Imagine that the reader is there in the story, seeing the visuals you've described. The description is "showing," and the explanation of the meaning behind the description is "telling." And often, what you've shown the readers gets the idea across even before you tell them. For example, consider this short paragraph:

> Red faced, he stomped across the floor and slammed his palm against the wall. "I want you out of here!" he shouted, leaning in menacingly close. He was obviously angry.

In this example, the man's actions—slamming the wall and stomping—as well as descriptions of his appearance—the red face—and plenty of his body language tell the readers he is angry. Also, shouting is often a good indicator of anger. So there's no need to state that he was angry when the description has set up a visual that conveys this information. In our daily lives, we don't have a narrator to follow us around, telling us motivations behind things we see. We have to infer motives and intentions from what our senses tell us.

Keep that in mind when you write. Take the readers to the place and show them the characters so that they can be in the moment with the character and experience those same moments.

"But," you might say, "what about when the description of the character is vague because I need to withhold info for now? How will the reader know what I mean?" Well, that's going to happen sometimes. Maybe the character laughs at an inappropriate moment, appears calm when he should be mad, or shows no outward signs of being surprised during unanticipated news. You might be tempted to explain these reactions, and you might be justified in that choice. However, if you're not careful, the need to explain a reaction might drag you into the trap of the accidental point-of-view shift, where you're telling the reader things that the point-of-view character wouldn't know. Consider this passage from a third-person point of view, where Jerry has just told the point-of-view character, Martha, of their ruined lab research:

> Surprised, Martha checked the results again. She couldn't believe that the sample had been contaminated. "How did this happen?" she cried, throwing the papers onto the desk. "That's months of work—gone!"
>
> Jerry shrugged, certain she didn't suspect him of espionage. She couldn't believe her usually quick-tempered partner was being so cool.

In this scene, Martha is very upset, and she has every reason to expect her partner to be just as upset as she is about the loss of their hard-earned research. That Jerry only shrugs seems out of the ordinary, especially since it's uncharacteristic of him. The temptation to explain his odd reaction has led into a description of Jerry's feelings, even though our point-of-view character, Martha, could not know how Jerry feels. That would require reading his mind, but if she *could* read his mind, this entire scene would go very differently. She would know exactly why he isn't as upset as she is. So to stick to a consistent point of view, we'll have to cut that bit where he's certain she didn't suspect him of espionage. The sentence that follows it shows that Martha doesn't know what's going on with Jerry, so even though the notion of espionage isn't mentioned, it's clear that she's not suspicious, only confused. Cutting the words doesn't cut the idea.

If Martha suspected Jerry of something dodgy without being certain of it, the author could describe Martha's suspicions from her point of view. Or if Martha noticed Jerry's body language that could have given him away, the author could show more of Jerry's outward appearance, even if Martha didn't make the connection:

> Surprised, Martha checked the results again. She couldn't believe that the sample had been contaminated. "How did this happen?" she cried, throwing the papers onto the desk. "That's months of work—gone!"
>
> Jerry shrugged. She couldn't believe her usually quick-tempered partner was being so cool, but he wouldn't look her in the eye. She wondered if he knew more than he was telling her.

There will be things that you, as the author, know you're going to reveal later in the story, but revealing them to the point-of-view character too soon would ruin the tension or even the entire story. If the point-of-view character doesn't know something, then maybe the reader shouldn't, either. You've chosen a particular character's point of view for a reason, and solving the mystery and making connections is part of the fun of reading a story. So it's okay to just give the reader the same clues you give the point-of-view character without delving into the meaning behind them too soon or too often.

Like ubiquitous ideas, which character is speaking can sometimes go without saying. Dialogue tags accompany dialogue and tell the reader who is speaking. Common dialogue tags include *he said* and *she asked*, but sometimes the reader doesn't need them to understand who is speaking. When the action that follows the dialogue obviously relates to the speaker of the dialogue, that tells readers who spoke. So the tag is unnecessary:

Clunky: "Let me look at that," Karen said, reaching for the cut above Jim's eyebrow.

He flinched. "Be careful," he told her.

Cleaner: "Let me look at that." Karen reached for the cut above Jim's eyebrow.

He flinched. "Be careful."

Karen's action tells us that she is speaking. It also tells us what she's talking about. So we really don't need "said." Jim's dialogue doesn't need a tag because he's obviously the one talking after the description of his flinching. And he must also be talking to Karen because his dialogue is a logical answer to her dialogue.

To avoid tangling up the dialogue when there's no tag, bump the dialogue to a new line when the dialogue switches characters. In the example below, Karen almost seems to be saying both pieces of dialogue. However, bumping Jim's action and dialogue to a new paragraph separates each character's actions and makes the flow of the conversation more intuitive.

Clunky:

"Here, let me look at that." Karen reached for the cut above Jim's eyebrow. He flinched. "Be careful."

Cleaner:

"Here, let me look at that." Karen reached for the cut above Jim's eyebrow.
He flinched. "Be careful."

Superfluous dialogue tags often accompany special punctuation such as em dashes and ellipses. So remember to make good use of punctuation and formatting, as well. Describing things that the punctuation tells us is usually redundant.

For example, em dashes mean the speaker was interrupted. So if another character's dialogue immediately follows an em dash, we know that this character interrupted the first speaker.

Polly took a deep breath before she spoke, which warned me this was going to be a long story. "So, first, I went to the dry cleaners, but they lost my pants. So then I went to Donna's to borrow—"
"That stinks," I said, interrupting her, "but did you get the package mailed on time?"

We don't need *interrupting her* because the em dash tells us that's what happened. Ellipses often share issues along these same lines. In dialogue, ellipses denote speech left unfinished because the idea wandered away before the speaker could voice it or because the speaker couldn't bear to or didn't know how to finish it. So you don't need to say the speaker *trailed off* when an ellipsis finishes the sentence.

These ideas apply to the narrative, as well as to dialogue. Ideas, especially in first-person point of view, might be interrupted or unfinished. And explaining what's going on isn't necessary because the punctuation makes that clear:

> As the plane hit turbulence, I grabbed my husband's hand. I thought about the girls and what they would do if—*no, don't think that way, Charlotte!*

In this example above, the narrator interrupts her own thoughts before she can finish, but in the example below, she simply trails off without completing the idea:

> As the plane hit turbulence, I grabbed my husband's hand. What would happen to the girls if we...

There's no need to add *I trailed off* or *I couldn't bear to finish* in the narrative because the ellipsis tells us so, and most readers will finish the thought on their own: what will happen to the girls if we crash... and, presumably, die? Dialogue would be treated the same way:

> As the plane hit turbulence, I grabbed my husband's hand. "What will happen to the girls if we..." I swallowed the lump in my throat.

Like punctuation, formatting can relay information that doesn't need further explanation. Many authors use italics to represent internal dialogue (when a character talks to himself or herself without actually voicing the words). Authors sometimes add "thought tags" (e.g., *she thought*) to internal dialogue. Paired with the use of italics, these thought tags can be superfluous. The first few times the point-of-view character has internal dialogue, the thought tag is okay, but once the italics are established as representing internal dialogue, you can drop things like *he thought* or *she wondered* when they follow direct thoughts. The example below, where we return to Martha and her devious lab partner, Jerry, presents inner dialogue in italics:

> Martha snatched the papers off the desk and stared at them again. *Contaminated? How could this happen?* she asked herself. She looked over at Jerry. *And why isn't he worried we're going to lose our jobs?*

In the example, *she asked herself* is a tag that describes the inner dialogue and thus establishes the formatting so that the second piece of inner dialogue doesn't need a tag. This use of italics can be especially handy in third-person narrative where the point of view is a little more distanced from the point-of-view character's perspective than first-person narrative is. But be careful of giving the italics too many jobs to do. If you've used italics for inner dialogue, avoid overusing it for emphasis, too. And remember, italics are very easy to overuse for emphasis. So italics are best used wisely and judiciously.

Plenty of descriptions relay information to the reader without requiring any further explanation, and showing an idea rather than simply explaining it pulls the reader into the story. Making effective use of punctuation and formatting makes your writing efficient, which means the reader gets to the good stuff more quickly.

CHAPTER 6:
ESTABLISHED AND IMPLIED IDEAS

This chapter goes beyond specific sentences and word choices to help you think about trimming excess material at the content level. To trim any established, obvious, or implied ideas, you'll need to think about your story in its entirety. Some things that warrant detailed descriptions at the beginning of a story don't need to be described again later on. The first description establishes the visual the reader will return to each time the location, person, piece of furniture—the list goes on and on—is involved in a scene.

Eye color, for example, is tempting to describe over and over. After a few mentions of the blue eyes, readers will get it—the guy has blue eyes. You might pepper in a few references to the already-established detail toward the middle and toward the end of the story, just as reminders, and keep the ones that are particularly eloquent. But look at your work really closely to decide between good writing and filler or words that just snuck in there. The same goes for descriptions like characters' complexion, hair color, weight, and clothing.

Experiences that are part of everyday life for most people also don't need tons of description. The average reader probably assumes the proper description anyway. Think of the sun, or perhaps the sunrise and sunset. The sun is ubiquitous. You can assume that most of your readers have seen the sun and understand, more or less, the concept. So even though you might describe the beauty of a sunset or sunrise, you don't really *need* to because your readers have likely already experienced it themselves. Of course, sunsets and sunrises can set the mood or inspire important feelings in the characters. Those passages are perfect for including a particularly eloquent description of a sunrise or sunset. Mundane things might become dramatic in certain moments, and descriptions of ubiquitous ideas are best saved for those moments.

Remember to consider your audience. Certain audiences have experience with different things. Will they need explanations of ideas to understand the story? Or could most of the people you expect to read your story be reasonably expected to follow along without an explanation?

For example, let's pretend you're writing a romance novel centered on characters who are in the military. Imagine your reader really enjoys the romance bits and likes the idea of the military stuff even if she doesn't have any real-life background knowledge of the military. You'll want your characters to use military jargon because that makes the story feel real and it's part of the character development. Your romance reader will know some of the lingo because she probably has acquaintances or family in the military, has seen television programs or movies about people in the military, and has possibly even read other military-based romance novels—she's reading this one, so that's not a wild expectation. Some of that stuff just floats around out there and sinks into people's heads.

Then you've got the stuff that your reader can easily figure out from context clues even if she doesn't know the background information. If you say the gun is loaded with enormous ammunition and makes a big boom, that's all she's going to need to know to understand that it does a lot of damage. And even if she doesn't know what a klick is when your romantic lead uses the word, she'll understand that he went pretty far if you imply that he covers a lot of ground.

And since you're writing a romance novel and not a straight-up military novel, the details can make the characters genuine, but the details about the machinery and the weaponry aren't why your romance reader will pick up the book. So even if those details are there and your reader isn't familiar with them, they don't necessarily warrant lots of explanation if those details don't affect the plot. Some things are obvious to different audiences, and others just won't concern them. For readers who are focused on the romance, not knowing the details about the military won't interfere with those readers' enjoyment of the story.

If those details are part of the plot or they serve as a clue, then they do warrant further explanation if your romance readers might not follow along with that information. If your main character spots something wrong with another character's uniform or body armor and this leads him or her to a conclusion—maybe he's a spy who didn't put the equipment on right—you might need to spell out the main character's thought process. The character might even work it out aloud or tell another character.

Or perhaps a malfunction with the ammunition gets someone killed. Rather than just showing the result of the malfunction, you might need to explain that what happened was unlikely, not just unexpected—and sabotage could be the cause. Readers who are into the romance bits of your story might not be all that familiar with the weaponry. However, if the additional details about the military aspects of the story are just there to set the scene and convey realism to the characters and their lives, you likely have little need to dive deep into explanations of those details.

Plenty of things are obvious to readers of any genre, though. And lots of those involve the point-of-view character's perception or POV. Beware of describing too much about how the point-of-view character perceives external stimuli by using the following phrases too often:

- he/she felt (could feel)

- he/she heard (could hear)

- he/she listened

- he/she saw (could see)

- he/she watched

When the point-of-view character describes a sound, he or she obviously heard that noise. Likewise, when the point-of-view character's description involves details of a visual, this character obviously saw whatever he or she is describing. The following examples show how to clean up these simple issues:

> **Clunky:** He saw the sun setting beyond the trees, like a giant ball of fire.

> **Cleaner:** Like a giant ball of fire, the sun set behind the trees.

> **Clunky:** She heard someone pounding on the door.

> **Cleaner:** Someone pounded on the door.

> **Clunky:** He felt his skin prickle as the hairy spider crawled up his arm.

> **Cleaner:** His skin prickled as the hairy spider crawled up his arm.

Always remember that in third-person or first-person narration, your narrative should not tell the reader things that the point-of-view character would not know; for example:

> Jimmy looked both ways before he crossed the street, but he didn't see the leggy blonde who was hiding behind the shrubbery of the neighbor's yard.

Because the point of view is attached to him, if Jimmy doesn't see this person, the narration can't offer up such a detailed description of her. Simply having him look both ways without describing seeing anyone *implies* Jimmy didn't see anything. The fix below sticks to the character's point of view while keeping all the important information, even the shrubbery that serves as the hiding place, in the sentence:

> Jimmy looked both ways before crossing the street, and the coast was clear—nothing but shrubbery.

Jimmy's story can also demonstrate how to avoid including too much description of how the point-of-view character perceives the things he or

Chapter 6: Established and Implied Ideas

she experiences. This example includes unnecessary information that tells the readers the information has been filtered through Jimmy's point of view:

> Jimmy watched the blonde stand up from behind the bushes. He could see that she was wearing a blue skirt that revealed her long legs. As he felt a cool breeze blow over his skin, he shivered. Then he heard her whistle for the dog standing in the adjacent yard.

Since Jimmy is our point-of-view character, and the narrative cannot describe things Jimmy doesn't know, then the reader can safely assume that Jimmy sees or watches all of the visuals described by the narrative. And he hears the sounds, tastes the tastes, and feels the sensations. The fix would go something like this:

> A blond woman stood up from behind the bushes. She was wearing a blue skirt that revealed her long legs. As a cool breeze blew over his skin, Jimmy shivered. Then the woman whistled for the dog standing in the adjacent yard.

And without all that extra sensory description bogging things down, it's clearer that we could go even further and do this:

> A leggy blonde wearing a revealing blue skirt stood up from behind the bushes. A cool breeze made Jimmy shiver. Then the woman whistled for the dog in the adjacent yard.

Since *blonde* can mean a woman with blond hair, that succinct noun can replace the description while keeping all the information. And *leggy* means having long legs. And a breeze must blow in order to be a breeze, so the idea that the air is moving is also covered. Jimmy would obviously use his skin to feel sensations like breezes. So moving things around and replacing longer descriptions tightens up wordiness without losing any of the ideas.

This same idea can also apply to information that a point-of-view character obviously knows or believes to be true. In both third-person and first-person narrative, the information in the story is limited to what the point-of-view character experiences, so everything that exists in the narration is obviously filtered through the lens of the point-of-view character, whoever that may be. Writers using omniscient third-person need to pay much closer attention

105

to this issue because the omniscient narration can move between characters' points of view. When using that narrative style, you might actually *need* to specify which character is using which senses to absorb the information readers receive in the narrative. It's also possible that none of the characters in the story see, hear, smell, or otherwise notice or experience certain things around them, even though the omniscient narrator did. So you'll have to be extra vigilant when deciding between redundancy and pertinent information. Writing in omniscient third-person point of view doesn't give you a free pass to spend too much time describing how the characters use their senses during the story.

Unless you're writing a piece using omniscient third-person narration, remember that the point-of-view character's assumptions, speculations, and opinions obviously color the presentation of everything in the narrative. So it's not always necessary to point out that the character knows the information you've stated in the narration or that the especially opinionated statements are based on his or her beliefs. When an idea is present in the narrative, it must have occurred to the point-of-view character, even if it is noticed subconsciously.

Clunky: He knew there were a million reasons he shouldn't go.

Cleaner: He had a million reasons not to go.

Clunky: To him, she seemed angry.

Cleaner: She seemed angry.

Clunky: In my opinion, she had a bad idea.

Cleaner: She had a bad idea.

The point-of-view character must notice everything that exists in the narration, even if its significance is not immediately apparent to that character. It's okay to slip clues into the narrative without delving deeper into the meaning behind them right away. Just let them be until the time comes to reveal the connection between the details that the point-of-view character notices and the overall story going on in the plot. For example, if our point-of-view character notices that her friend Sarah changed clothes during a party, she doesn't have to jump to the conclusion right then that Sarah just murdered her boyfriend out back and had to jettison her bloody shirt—even if that's what happened. The point-of-view character doesn't even have to speculate at all. Readers will accept that there's an explanation for something so commonplace, even if one isn't given in the moment. If they haven't spilled drinks on themselves at a party, they've seen someone who has. So that perfectly reasonable explanation is already floating around in their minds. If you're not ready to reveal the crime, you can simply drop the clue by mentioning the wardrobe change then moving on.

Many other clues also work best when the readers aren't stuck in a scene where the same information gets repeated over and over. Certain aspects of characters or places are easily described too often, especially when they're meant to set the scene. For example, if part of the story takes place in a mansion—and the mere usage of *mansion* implies that the setting is lavish— and if you've established that the furnishings are extravagant, there's no need to continue to describe *each* of the objects the characters encounter in the mansion as opulent, expensive, luxurious, and the like. The contents of the mansion would presumably suit the standard of wealth presented by the mansion. However, if the furnishings are unusually cheap or out of place, then the repeated description of the inside of the mansion becomes important to setting the stage and delving deeper into the plot or characters who live in the mansion.

Characters' physical traits, like the eye color I mentioned at the beginning of this chapter, easily become repetitive, as well. For example, if you've described a character's tan complexion near the beginning, it's an established visual. It doesn't bear repeating a bunch of times. It might be worth mentioning when he's standing near particularly pale people if his tan makes others seem sickly by comparison or another situation where it offers up information. If this man has a dark complexion, but his relatives do not, this might be a clue that he is adopted or has been traveling somewhere sunny. But if that's just his complexion, relay the information then move on.

Some points warrant explanation, while others will be obvious to most readers. Consider whom you're writing for. Depending on the audience, certain ideas do not need to be explained because the readers will know and understand them, the readers will not need to understand in order to enjoy the story, or the information simply exists in another form. Remember that the visual you've created often implies what you want the readers to know. If it's a clue, it could be worth repeating or pointing out, but don't go overboard on the details if you've already set the scene.

CHAPTER 7:
PROFESSIONAL PEEVES

As an editor, I have a few professional pet peeves. These include a few things I think should be described sparingly—or perhaps not at all. The following discussion serves mostly to get you really thinking about what aspects of your writing might have gone off on a tangent. This list doesn't represent anything and everything that might distract a reader or detract from the storyline. However, it does offer up a few examples of filler that commonly sneaks into books and examples of the kinds of things that are sometimes left over after rewrites that took characters and stories in a new direction. Readers enjoy participating in the experience of reading a story, and they like coming to their own conclusions. This often leaves authors to walk a fine line between dishing out the important information and stranding the reader in a swamp of details.

Being too detailed about house or apartment layouts can be tedious. The readers don't necessarily need to be able to navigate the dwelling alone. After all, they'll be with the narrator if they go anywhere. So there's little need to describe it so well that readers could draw their own layouts. They need to know if it's cramped or spacious. They might need to know the placement of a few key items or rooms, including whether they are downstairs or upstairs. If the decorations are particularly ghastly or somehow reflect the personality of the person who lives there, then give that description. Or if the place is in disrepair, show that. Beyond that, just let the reader build his or her own visual.

The exceptions to this rule are if the layout and details of a location are key to solving a mystery or if the layout is plot related. If a sneaky operation is afoot, readers might need to know more than usual about the layout to understand the proximity of the perpetrators to the person who is unaware of their presence. You should also hit the highlights of the appearance of the setting if those things relate important details. For example, if the place hasn't been used in a while, you might describe the tattered, faded curtains and dusty cobwebs. But if your description is obviously describing an abandoned place, you don't need to explicitly say that no one has been there for a while. This involves a bit of the "show and tell" discussed in Chapter 5. In the end, the reader should be able to picture the location, not draw a blueprint.

Overdescription of rooms and houses can be particularly frustrating because, as a reader, I try to remember these things, thinking they will be important later on. When an author makes a point of saying a door is closed when it should have been open, I think there might be an intruder behind it. Or perhaps a ghost is in residence. I expect this specific inclusion to serve the plot. When these details turn out to be simply heavy description, I feel as though I wasted energy that I could have expended on other aspects of the book that did matter. And I suspect other readers feel the same. Especially in mysteries, beware the *accidental* red herring.

Also be careful of food descriptions. The reader doesn't always need to know specifically what the characters are eating or how they cooked it. The mundane parts of characters' lives are expected even if an author doesn't discuss them. Eating is one of those mundane things. However, food *can* be part of character development. For example, if your narrator takes special care preparing her grandmother's favorite recipe or if she whips something up just like her mother did, it bears mentioning because it's part of who she is. Scenes set in a restaurant might involve food details that provide pertinent information. Did the narrator's date order her something? That matters because it tells us something about the date's personality or the nature of their relationship. Is it too heavy for an upset stomach? This tells us that the character is not feeling well.

Keep in mind that readers will try to ascribe importance to just about anything you tell them. As a reader, I assume the author has kept it to the important stuff. Did you describe the food and make mention of pickles because she's pregnant and craving pickles? Or did she just need a quick snack? If you make a big deal mentioning the soda water, I'll assume she had a queasy stomach.

Steer clear of the temptation to describe the food at every single meal. You don't need to seemingly starve the characters, but saying something like they had "a quick lunch" or "a bite to eat" will often suffice for those meals that didn't take long and don't factor in to the plot. And there's almost never a reason to get down to the nitty-gritty of the actual plate presentation. I could imagine scenarios in which one of the characters is a master chef, and these descriptions might come into play then. Or perhaps the plot might involve food allergies or a poisoned character. Otherwise, unless you're talking about something like fried spiders or chocolate-covered grasshoppers, try to keep descriptions of food to a minimum, with allowances for characters' specialty dishes, plot-driven dishes, and stomach-churning moments.

Similarly, don't go overboard in identifying where people are standing or sitting—unless there's a fight about to break out, and readers need to know that Guy A is standing close enough for Guy B to kick him in the face, jab him in the groin, or otherwise damage him through the use of bodily contact. He might be standing too far away to suddenly touch the other man, but it also won't matter much unless he *wants* to touch that other guy.

When your characters *do* throw down, try to remember that readers will care more about the impact and outcome of the fight than they will about the choreography. Don't get mired in the exact details of every strike and parry. Readers who aren't familiar with martial arts or who don't find themselves in many brawls are probably going to skim over the mechanics of the fight to get to the result. You also risk frustrating those readers who are martial artists and might perceive a flaw—imagined or not—in your choreography. You can hit a nice middle ground by sticking with the blows that affect the outcome or cause lasting injuries.

Sometimes, the fighting is more mental than physical. Maybe the female lead gets stuck sitting next to her arch nemesis at a dinner party. Or maybe the usually happy couple haven't gone near each other during the entire party. Those instances warrant pointing out because these proximities offer insight about the characters' feelings.

But if everyone is more or less just standing around or hanging out, just say so. Knowing who is next to whom isn't important unless that's important to the story. And when it is important, pay special attention to the flow of your information. Mysteries often make use of establishing where everyone is sitting because it serves as a clue or a red herring. But be careful of throwing the reader off the trail accidentally. Also pay special attention to scenes that involve more than, say, three or four characters because the setup can quickly spiral out of control. Setup for scenes that describe where too many characters are standing can read like an info dump if the description isn't interwoven with small insights about the placement of the characters. Always avoid just listing from left to right who is standing where.

Driving directions can also be frustrating for readers who are not overly familiar with the book's precise geographic setting. As a reader, when I run into a long list of which roads or streets the characters are using, I'm often at a loss for what I should be taking away from that information. Repairing this misdirection is often more about making better use of descriptions than cutting them. Instead of driving instructions, give the reader an indication of the environment the characters are driving through. Is it a nice neighborhood where they don't fit in? Is it a run-down neighborhood where they feel they're about to be accosted? Is it a shortcut or somewhere that they are likely to hit traffic? Sometimes authors go beyond simply missing the point and even expect readers to make conclusions based on street or road names without filling in the blanks; for example:

> I dashed into the break room to grab a cup of coffee before the
> meeting. I'd taken Elm Street through to Sixth. So, naturally, I was
> running late for work. Everyone at the conference table turned
> to look at me when I opened the door.

In this case, the author has expected the reader to make a connection between the streets the narrator chose and the reason he was late for work. But to readers who are unfamiliar with these streets, the reason could be nearly anything. Are these roads prone to traffic jams? Did he have to stop for a herd of sheep to cross? Was there road construction? Did he pass in front of a restaurant where delivery trucks tend to be stopped in the street to make deliveries? If the narrator's lateness warrants explanation, that's just as easily accomplished by skipping the street names and telling the reason:

I dashed into the break room to grab a cup of coffee before the meeting. I'd hit traffic on the way to work, so I was running late. Everyone at the conference table turned to look at me when I opened the door.

The issues in this section do tread the fine line between too much telling and not enough showing, but be careful of too much showing, as well. Too-detailed descriptions can often lead readers down a trail of confusion or boredom if they can't sort out what's important. Following the above suggestions will help you avoid creating that situation in your book.

WRAP-UP AND QUIZ

Getting to the point isn't all about cutting word count. It's about making the words count. And no advice is right every single time in every situation. But as a rule of thumb, don't be afraid to cut. If you've cut so much that you feel as if you have nothing left but a story, you've probably cut just the right amount. The story is what you came to tell. You obviously want it to sound good and make sense, but anything that doesn't enhance the writing doesn't serve you, your plot, or the reader's experience.

Beyond avoiding verbosity and redundant wording, ideas, and description, you need to take careful stock of your writing to be certain that it's helping the story. To do that, it should push the plot forward, be part of character development, establish important background information, set the scene, or build the world. A story often takes shape after several revisions, and it's important to keep a special lookout for things that might have been important in the first draft but became unnecessary in the final draft. Keeping the clutter to a minimum by leaving out redundant wording and wordiness in the beginning should help make the other, broader redundancies and unnecessary descriptions more apparent. And once you've trimmed those, you'll have just the good stuff left.

The following quiz will help you practice getting to the point. Each question recreates one of the issues I've discussed in this book. Rewrite and revise the sentences to avoid those issues. You'll find the answers, along with an explanation of the answers, at the end of the quiz.

QUIZ

1. Jennifer's cheeks turned crimson red before she looked away.

2. It was Alex who finally decided to pull the cord at the last minute, with no time to spare.

3. As he contemplated his answer, Bob nodded his head. He shrugged his shoulders before answering, "I think so."

4. The sun looked as though it were a fire on the horizon.

5. Sharon's dress made her look as though she were a lollipop.

6. Stephen was injured when he rear-ended a car he was following behind.

7. "Are you feeling well?" Katherine asked, concerned, as she rested the back of her hand against his forehead.

8. The object in the corner of the dark room seemed to be almost glowing a little.

9. Feeling like a drowned rat, she imagined she looked like a Popsicle melting in the rain.

10. She wore a pink scarf around her neck, and she clung to it tightly.

11. It was Jim's idea to try the sushi.

12. There was a room at the end of the hall that drew my attention.

13. My grammar was corrected by my teacher during class.

14. He complained about having to pick up the crayons that had been spilled by the other kids during lunch.

15. Laura gripped the remote tightly, afraid the bomb would explode if she took her finger off of the trigger.

QUIZ ANSWERS

1.

Original: Jennifer's cheeks turned crimson red before she looked away.

Edited: Jennifer's cheeks turned crimson before she looked away.

The original description doubled up on the color. Even though red might come in shades other than crimson, crimson is always a shade of red. So that extra *red* isn't necessary.

2.

Original: It was Alex who finally decided to pull the cord at the last minute, with no time to spare.

Edited: Alex finally decided to pull the cord at the last minute.

> **Or:** With no time to spare, Alex finally decided to pull the cord.

The original sentence suffered from wordiness. Several of those words simply weren't needed. And there are a few ways to fix the repetition. *At the last minute* and *with no time to spare* say the same thing twice, but with different words. Keeping either is fine, but not both.

3.

Original: As he contemplated his answer, Bob nodded his head. He shrugged his shoulders before answering, "I think so."

Edited: As he contemplated his answer, Bob nodded. He shrugged. "I think so."

This wording was redundant because nodding, by definition, involves the head. The same goes for shrugging and shoulders. You can also trim the dialogue tag *before answering* because the order in which the action was presented tells the reader that Bob shrugged before he spoke.

4.

Original: The sun looked as though it were a fire on the horizon.

Edited: The sun looked like a fire on the horizon.

   Or: The sun set fire to the horizon.

Use a metaphor or a simile to cut some wordiness. It's okay, really. This will give your writing more panache.

5.

Original: Sharon's dress made her look as though she were a lollipop.

Edited: Sharon's dress made her look like a lollipop.

Use *like* instead of *as though*. The proper use of the preposition *like* compares a noun to a noun (or a gerund to a gerund). The original sentence compared a person (noun) to a state of being (looking like a lollipop). The state of being is how something is, not *what* it is.

6.

Original: Stephen was injured when he rear-ended a car he was following behind.

Edited: Stephen was injured when he rear-ended a car.

Beware of overstating the obvious. A car that rear-ends another would obviously be following that first car. And *following* is by definition *behind*. It's also safe to assume the reader will understand that this car was in an accident with another *car*. To be fair, it's possible that a horse-drawn carriage or a motorcycle could have been involved in the accident, but that would be exactly the kind of thing the author should tell us. If there's no identification of the other vehicle involved, the reader will assume what is most familiar or what likely happened.

7.

Original: "Are you feeling well?" Katherine asked, concerned, as she rested the back of her hand against his forehead.

Edited: "Are you feeling well?" Katherine rested the back of her hand against his forehead.

Because Katherine's action follows the dialogue so closely, this tells us that she was the one who spoke. So *asked* is a superfluous dialogue tag. We also know that she asked a question because of the punctuation in the dialogue. And the fact that she asked at all and that she made a comforting and concerned gesture in touching his forehead shows that she was concerned.

8.

Original: The object in the corner of the dark room seemed to be almost glowing a little.

Edited: The object in the corner of the dark room seemed to be glowing.

The original sentence included lots of hedging. *Glowing* doesn't really describe something that is shining brightly anyway, so backing away from the description with so many qualifiers—*seemed to be, almost, a little*—isn't necessary. Don't pull away from a description; just go for it and get it in there.

9.

Original: Feeling like a drowned rat, she imagined she looked like a Popsicle melting in the rain.

Edited: She felt like a drowned rat and imagined she looked like one, too.

Or: She imagined she looked like a Popsicle melting in the rain.

This one has lots of possible fixes, just as long as they don't include both the Popsicle and the rat. These descriptions both more or less describe the same idea: the woman is wet, and she feels uncomfortable about it. Using two descriptions for the same visual draws away from each of them, especially because the two visuals are so very different. They do not build on each other. Let one take center stage and carry the idea. That will make the visual stronger.

10.

Original: She wore a pink scarf around her neck, and she clung to it tightly.

Edited: She clung tightly to the pink scarf around her neck.

The original was simply too wordy. Combining the ideas into a single concise sentence tells us all the same information, and the tighter sentence reads more smoothly.

11.

Original: It was Jim's idea to try the sushi.

Edited: Trying the sushi was Jim's idea.

Clean up the common clunker (*it was*) with a gerund.

12.

Original: There was a room at the end of the hall that drew my attention.

Edited: The room at the end of the hall drew my attention.

The clunker (*there was*) runs off with the sentence. Using *there was* traps the sentence into an unnecessarily wordy structure.

The shorter version offers up just as much information as the original without employing the clunky structure.

13.

Original: My grammar was corrected by my teacher during class.

Edited: My teacher corrected my grammar during class.

Switching from passive voice to active tightens up the sentence and makes it clearer.

14.

Original: He complained about having to pick up the crayons that had been spilled by the other kids during lunch.

Edited: He complained about having to pick up the crayons the other kids had spilled during lunch.

In the original, the second part of the sentence was in passive voice. Changing *the crayons that had been spilled by the other kids* to *the crayons the other kids had spilled* repairs the passive voice. The change also moves the verb (*spilled*) closer to the words that describe when that verb happened (*during lunch*), and that makes for a sturdier sentence.

15.

Original: Laura gripped the remote tightly, afraid the bomb would explode if she took her finger off of the trigger.

Edited: Laura gripped the remote tightly, afraid the bomb would explode if she took her finger off the trigger.

The word *of* should not follow *off*.

ABOUT THE AUTHOR

Stefanie Spangler Buswell has a bachelor of arts from Western Illinois University, and she tried out a few other careers before settling down to read books for a living. Books and reading have always been her passion. So she's excited to be a part of creating great books.

Stefanie lives in central Illinois with her husband and daughter. She is currently the executive publisher assistant and a line editor at Red Adept Publishing. When she's not editing, she enjoys gardening, knitting, and forcing others to read her favorite books.

BEYOND the STYLE MANUAL

RED ADEPT PUBLISHING

HE SAID, SHE SAID
WRITING EFFECTIVE DIALOGUE

INTRODUCTION

Of all the elements of writing, dialogue can be one of the trickiest to get just right. It can also be one of the least forgiving if you get it wrong. Writing fiction is always an exercise in balancing a sense of realism with the artistic conventions of telling a story through words on a page, and dialogue, because it purports to represent what people really sound like, can test a writer's ability to perform that balancing act.

Unlike some aspects of writing, dialogue has few hard and fast rules. Once you've mastered the conventions of the punctuation used to represent dialogue on the page, the "rules" for writing dialogue become more like suggestions. But some of those suggestions will serve you well in trying to write dialogue that will sound "like real people" while still reading like good writing. For every suggestion outlined in this manual, you will be able to find at least one lauded writer who is famous for a style that ignores or even flouts that suggestion. But if you're aiming for good, realistic, readable dialogue that breathes life into your story, following the guidelines in this manual will set you on your way.

This manual will lay out those guidelines, helping you get your dialogue on the page, teaching you how to integrate your dialogue into your narrative, and giving you tips on how to strike that important balance between realism and style in your dialogue. Finally, the last chapter provides exercises for you to practice your dialogue, along with discussions of those exercises.

1:
PUTTING DIALOGUE ON THE PAGE

HOW DIALOGUE SHOULD LOOK ON THE PAGE

One of the keys to writing effective dialogue is ensuring that your dialogue appears on the page in a way that is easy to read and will let your reader know that it is dialogue without drawing undue attention to itself. While this section will not go into the particulars of all the various little tricks of punctuation that can arise in writing dialogue, it is important to understand a few basics regarding how dialogue is traditionally presented.

The presentation of dialogue on the page has varied over time—and still does vary from country to country—but in U.S. publishing, dialogue is typically indicated by double quotation marks (" "), with the opening quotation mark (") appearing at the beginning of a line of dialogue and the closing quotation mark (") appearing at the end.

A dialogue tag may be used to identify which character spoke the line. The dialogue tag must consist of at least a noun (indicating the speaker of the dialogue) and a verb (indicating the action denoting speech). The dialogue tag is separated from the dialogue with a comma. A line of dialogue followed by a dialogue tag looks like this:

> *"Nothing suits me better than a fried egg on toast early in the morning," Billy said.*

The tag can also appear before the dialogue, in which case the comma moves with it, like so:

> Billy said, "Nothing suits me better than a fried egg on toast early in the morning."

In addition to being set off with quotation marks, dialogue is often indicated through paragraphing. In a dialogue exchange, begin a new paragraph each time a different character speaks:

> Billy and John walked into the kitchen.
>
> "Nothing suits me better than a fried egg on toast early in the morning," Billy said.
>
> "Not me," John said. "I can't stand anything but a cup of coffee until at least twelve o'clock."

Actions taken by a character just before, just after, or during his dialogue should appear in the same paragraph as his dialogue. Actions taken by other characters in the scene should appear in a new paragraph (along with their dialogue, if they have any):

> Billy and John walked into the kitchen.
>
> "Nothing suits me better than a fried egg on toast early in the morning," Billy said. He opened a cupboard, looking for a frying pan.
>
> John made a face. "Not me. I can't stand anything but a cup of coffee until at least twelve o'clock."

If only one character speaks a line of dialogue but both characters have actions in the scene, put the nonspeaking character's actions in a new paragraph, just as you would if he had dialogue as well:

Billy and John walked into the kitchen.

"Nothing suits me better than a fried egg on toast early in the morning," Billy said.

John made a face.

"What? Don't you like eggs?" Billy asked.

John shook his head. "Not first thing in the morning, no."

Following these few simple guidelines will help ensure that your dialogue is presented clearly on the page.

DIALOGUE TAGS

A dialogue tag is used to identify which character spoke a line of dialogue. Tags should always include a verb that indicates speech and should not draw attention to themselves. A dialogue tag's primary (and often only) function is to identify who's speaking, and therefore it is usually best to allow the tags to disappear into the background of your writing. To this end, think of the tags "said" and "asked" as your default tags. Many situations will call for other tags (and we'll look at those situations shortly), but if there is no good reason to use a tag other than "said" or "asked," use them. While in most other aspects of writing, vivid and varied verbs are a good way to improve your prose, dialogue tags other than "said" and "asked" may draw unwanted attention to the tags. A reader will absorb "said" and "asked" almost without realizing it, and the dialogue tag will therefore do its job of identifying the speaker without disrupting the narrative or throwing the reader out of the story.

Verbs that indicate at what volume or in what manner a character spoke are wonderful as tags if used sparingly and only when it is important to plot or characterization to do so. Such verbs include "shouted," "yelled," "whispered," "murmured," and "muttered." For the most part, avoid drafting verbs that do not refer to speech into use as dialogue tags—verbs such as "blurted," "ejaculated," "announced," "protested," "interrupted," "continued," "repeated," "answered," and "commented." While some of the verbs often drafted into use as dialogue tags are objectionable only from the point of view of writing craft, many of them are actually grammatically suspect. Verbs that do not directly identify speech are often transitive verbs. Transitive verbs require direct objects (a noun that can "receive" the action of the verb) in order to express an action completely. Intransitive verbs do not require a direct object; they express actions completely on their own.

- Some intransitive verbs in sentences:

He walked.

She slept.

The cat meowed.

Dan jumped.

- Some transitive verbs in sentences:

He threw the ball.

She hugged her brother.

Dan carried the shopping bag.

"Said" and "asked" are both transitive verbs; they require objects. In a line of dialogue with a tag, the dialogue itself functions as the object of the transitive verb "said" or "asked." However, when you use another transitive verb as your tag (one that is not conventionally used as a dialogue tag), the verb may seem incomplete. It may *seem* as if it is missing its object even if it can take the dialogue itself as its object. Consider "to blurt," a transitive verb that is sometimes used in dialogue tags:

>   *She blurted her answer.*

>   *"Fourteen," she blurted.*

While "blurted" takes the dialogue itself as its object (just as "said" and "asked" would), readers may be less used to seeing "blurted" without an object following it and may stumble over the line. Since you want those tags to disappear into the background, making the reader stumble is never a good idea. Other transitive verbs used in tags don't work that well:

>   *Margie interrupted her.*

>   *"I don't think that's a good idea," Margie interrupted.*

If you flipped the sentence with "blurted" around, you have a sentence that works as we usually expect one with a transitive verb to work: *She blurted, "Fourteen"* works very similarly to *She blurted her answer.* But *Margie interrupted, "I don't think that's a good idea"* is not analogous to *Margie interrupted her* because *"I don't think that's a good idea"* isn't what Margie interrupted while *"her"* is. It's best to avoid those unconventional transitive verbs in dialogue tags altogether. (If you think a verb sounds a little wonky in a dialogue tag and you aren't sure if it's transitive, check a dictionary. Dictionary entries for verbs will tell you if the verb is transitive or intransitive.)

Any verbs not directly related to speech may draw attention to themselves as dialogue tags (possibly throwing the reader out of the story), and worse, they often indicate that the writer has asked the tag to do too much work. Dialogue tags identify speakers and may indicate something about the speech itself, nothing more. Do not ask them also to show the reader how the character feels, or how he sounds, or what he's going to do next. Show the reader those things through characterization and action. Do not unintentionally state the obvious through the tag by telling the reader something she should have picked up from the narrative. If Billy asks John a question and John answers the question, the act itself tells the reader that John answered the question. It is not necessary to use the dialogue tag to tell the reader that John answered Billy:

"What? Don't you like eggs?" Billy asked.

"Not first thing in the morning, no," John answered.

In this example, the verb "answered" in the dialogue tag isn't necessary. The reader can see that John has answered the question, so stating that he's answered it is redundant. (One might argue that "said" and "asked" are redundant in the same way, but it is sometimes necessary to attribute a line of dialogue to a character, and "said" and "asked" are generally the best way to do that without drawing too much attention to the redundancy.) If you use "said" and "asked" as your default tags, they will fade into the background, and readers will pick up on the character name without having to focus on the verb following.

Because you want your dialogue tags to disappear into the background, it is also a good idea to use a noun–verb construction for dialogue tags rather than a verb–noun construction. In other words, put the character's name first and the verb second:

"Not first thing in the morning, no," John said.

rather than

"Not first thing in the morning, no," said John.

The most important piece of information in the dialogue tag will always be who is speaking. Put that first so the reader can skip over and quickly absorb the verb, which, in a way, is only there for completeness's sake.

WHEN TO USE A DIALOGUE TAG

Think of dialogue tags almost as you would punctuation: without punctuation, your writing would be nearly impossible to follow, and it's important to use punctuation correctly. But if the punctuation is doing its job, readers will hardly notice it. The same is true of dialogue tags; you want your readers to hardly notice them. Aside from the tricks for making your tags disappear that

I mentioned above, one of the best ways to ensure your readers don't notice your tags is to be sure you know when (and when not) to use them.

Remembering that a dialogue tag's primary function is to identify the speaker will help you immeasurably here. The first question to ask yourself is: "Is it clear who is speaking without a tag?" If the answer is yes, you may be able to go without the tag altogether. The next question to ask is: "How many lines of dialogue has it been since a character was identified by a tag?" (or an action—more on identifying speaking characters through actions in a bit). If it's been more than four lines without a definitive identification of who is speaking, it's time for a tag.

In this example, notice how in the line without a tag there's no question who's speaking:

> *Miranda leaned over the kitchen counter with a pastry bag, trying to write "Happy Birthday Marty" on a cake with little success.*
>
> *Ben yanked open the top drawer of the sideboard and stared at the array of colorful napkins folded neatly inside before leaning back to look into the kitchen. "Which set did you want?" he asked.*
>
> *"The blue ones."*

Since Ben and Miranda are the only two characters in this scene and the paragraphing and situation both suggest that the line *"The blue ones"* is not spoken by Ben, readers will understand without a tag that the line must have been spoken by Miranda. In situations like this one, avoid using an unnecessary tag.

However, if Ben and Miranda's exchange goes on for several lines without any identifying action to indicate who speaks which lines, add a tag even if the reader could easily figure out which line belongs to which character. The tag helps avoid confusion and allows the reader to carry on with the scene without having to backtrack to be sure they know who said what:

Ben yanked open the top drawer of the sideboard and stared at the array of colorful napkins folded neatly inside. "Which set did you want?" he called to Miranda, who was trying to write "Happy Birthday Marty" on a cake with little success.

"The blue ones!"

"Which ones?"

"The blue ones!"

"I like the yellow ones."

"Marty hates yellow."

"No, he doesn't," Ben said. "He has that mustardy pair of socks. And that sweater that looks like a dandelion sneezed on it."

In addition to avoiding using a tag when one is not necessary, you can also reduce the overall number of tags in your writing by identifying speaking characters in other ways aside from putting a tag at the end of their dialogue. If characters act or gesture just before or after their line of dialogue, the reader will know that that dialogue belongs to that character, even without a dialogue tag. Consider this line:

Will flopped onto the couch and rested his feet on the edge of the coffee table. "Say, this place isn't too bad," he said.

The tag after Will's dialogue isn't necessary. It's clear from the paragraphing that the line belongs to Will. (Remember that a character's actions occurring just before or just after a line of dialogue should appear in the same paragraph as the dialogue itself.) In situations like this, simply eliminate the tag and allow the character's action to identify him as the speaker:

> *Will flopped onto the couch and rested his feet on the edge of the coffee table. "Say, this place isn't too bad."*

This technique works equally well in long dialogue exchanges. You may find that you can write an entire dialogue exchange without ever using a tag at all:

> *Will flopped onto the couch and rested his feet on the edge of the coffee table. "Say, this place isn't too bad."*
>
> *"It's really not." Tom nudged Will's feet to the floor. "And I'd like to keep it that way."*
>
> *Will looked around the small living room and craned his head to try to see into the adjoining kitchen. "What kind of rent do you pay on a place like this?"*
>
> *Tom looked down the short hall to his tiny bedroom, as if he might find the answer lurking there. "Too much."*

While actions accompanying dialogue are an excellent way to avoid overusing tags, take care not to let the presentation of those actions become repetitive. Remember to vary the placement of actions within dialogue exchanges. An action might come before the line of dialogue, or after it, or in the middle of it, especially if one character speaks more than one sentence at a time. Avoid exchanges like this, where all the identifying actions occur before the lines of dialogue:

> *Elizabeth sat primly on the edge of her seat. "The weather has been quite fine these past few days."*
>
> *Charles fiddled with the buttons on his jacket. "Yes. I thought I might go hiking this weekend if it stays nice."*
>
> *Elizabeth added another lump of sugar to her coffee. "That sounds fun."*

> *Charles clenched his fists to keep his fingers away from those stupid buttons. "It should be."*

Make the scene livelier simply by varying the placement of the characters' actions:

> *Elizabeth sat primly on the edge of her seat. "The weather has been quite fine these past few days."*

> *"Yes." Charles fiddled with the buttons on his jacket. "I thought I might go hiking this weekend if it stays nice."*

> *"That sounds fun." Elizabeth added another lump of sugar to her coffee.*

> *Charles clenched his fists to keep his fingers away from those stupid buttons. "It should be."*

All of the examples I have provided so far include only two characters in each dialogue exchange. You will likely need more tags when you have a scene involving three or more characters, since a response to any one character might come from a number of other characters. In these situations, remember the power of actions (instead of tags) as identifiers, but be sure to use dialogue tags whenever necessary to avoid confusion. When writing a scene with more than two characters, it is often tempting to indicate that some dialogue was said to or asked of one character in particular:

> *"I've never liked that tie of your father's," Mrs. Wythe said to Cyril. "See if you can get him to change it."*

or

> *"Are you coming with us?" Doris asked her.*

This construction is highly useful when it is necessary to avoid confusion, but like dialogue tags in general, it should not be overused. Never use this construction if the identity of the character being addressed is clear without it, and avoid it at all costs in scenes between only two people. You can avoid this construction in the same ways you can avoid dialogue tags. Actions as identifiers, for example, can indicate to whom a line is addressed, even if there are many characters in a scene:

> *Mrs. Wythe smiled at her guests sitting round the breakfast table. Without changing her expression in the slightest, she patted Cyril's hand and leaned toward him. "I've never liked that tie of your father's. See if you can get him to change it."*

Similarly, report that a character spoke "to herself" only if it will otherwise be unclear that her dialogue was not addressed to other characters in the scene. If Jenny is alone in her room and speaking dialogue, she must be speaking to herself, so it's not necessary to say she is:

> *Jenny slammed the door of her bedroom so hard that the picture of her and her brothers at the lake fell over on her nightstand. She threw her book bag at her desk chair then flopped onto the bed. "It's not fair. All that planning, all my planning, ruined. Just ruined." She toed off her shoes and kicked one of them toward the closet. "All because he can't be bothered to help."*

But if there's someone else in the room with Jenny and she's not really talking to that person, you may need to indicate that:

> *Jenny slammed the door of her bedroom so hard that her sister jumped. She threw her book bag at her desk chair then flopped onto the bed. "It's not fair," she said, more to herself than to her sister. "All that planning, all my planning, ruined. Just ruined." She toed off her shoes and kicked one of them toward the closet. "All because he can't be bothered to help."*

HOW TO STOP ASKING TAGS TO DO TOO MUCH

Let's take another look at one kind of undesirable dialogue tag I mentioned earlier. I said to avoid overusing verbs other than "said" and "asked" in your tags because doing so sometimes asks your tag to do too much work. Consider this line of dialogue:

"But I wanted to go with you!" Sally blurted.

The verb "blurted" tries to tell the reader an awful lot about what's going on with Sally. "To blurt" is to say something suddenly and probably without thinking about the consequences first, and on the face of it, it seems as if this verb should be okay to use in a tag. It does, after all, indicate speech and say something about the manner of the speech (in the way that "whisper" or "shouted" would). But more is packed into that verb than should be. When Sally "blurts" out her line of dialogue, that verb is being asked to stand in for development of Sally's feelings and thoughts. Without any further indication of what Sally looks like, what she's doing, or how she's feeling, that "blurt" is being asked to carry too much weight. It would be better to show the reader all that is behind "blurt":

Sally looked from her father to her brother, her eyes wide. They couldn't be planning to cut her out of their plans this way. "But I wanted to go with you!"

While editing out the "blurt" tag does mean that the line loses the explicit sense of "saying something suddenly without considering the consequences," the description of Sally (her wide eyes, the way she looks from father to brother) and the access to her feelings (disbelief at their actions) suggest the kind of state in which she might not be thinking about consequences. And the exclamation point in her dialogue itself suggests she spoke "suddenly." Unpacking what is meant by the less ideal tag "blurt" allows for more description and a fuller evocation of character—without having to use the tag at all.

This same kind of packing too much into one word can also occur if you rely too heavily on adverbs or adjectives within your dialogue tags. An adverb describes a verb, adjective, or another adverb, and an adjective modifies or describes a noun. Here are some examples of dialogue tags containing an adverb:

"I want ice cream," Maise said petulantly.

"I think I might love you," Jamie said softly.

"Clean up your crap," Alan said irritably.

These examples show dialogue tags including an adjective:

"I hate when you do that," Moira said, annoyed.

"I just love the snow," Lindsey said, delighted.

You want to take care not to overuse adverbs or adjectives with dialogue tags for the same reason you want to avoid dialogue tags other than "said" and "asked"—they often indicate that you are relying too heavily on telling the reader things rather than showing her. Instead of saying that Alan is irritable, show that he is by describing him or his actions:

Alan tripped over his roommate's book bag for the third time that afternoon. He snatched the bag up by one strap and shook it in Tim's direction. "For the last time! Clean up your crap."

The situation here and the additional dialogue (*"For the last time!"*) paint a picture of irritability that means the adverb (and the tag itself) aren't necessary. Instead of telling the reader that Lindsey is delighted, show that delight:

Lindsey cupped her mittened hands in front of her, watching as flake after flake hit her hands and melted slowly into the stitching. She tipped her head back and twirled. "I just love the snow."

The description of how Lindsey behaves in the snow illustrates her delight without the writer having to say she is delighted.

Sometimes, adverbs in dialogue tags are useful. The ones that describe the manner of speech (such as "softly" in the example with Jamie above) often add something important to the scene and frequently can't be described easily. Avoid using any of these adverbs too often (because any kind of overrepetition makes for dull writing), but don't be afraid to use them when they are appropriate to your scene. Adverbs that describe the character who is speaking or how that character is feeling or what their state of being is (adverbs like "cheerfully," "gravely," "carefully," "grumpily," "patiently," "purposefully") are best avoided in dialogue tags. These are the adverbs that are being asked to do too much work. Replace them with telling descriptions of the character or his actions. Adjectives in tags are similarly useful and sometimes necessary, but consider whether replacing them with description will bring your character and your scene more fully to life.

AVOIDING POINT-OF-VIEW PROBLEMS IN DIALOGUE TAGS

When you begin to add things on to your dialogue tags (such as adverbs or adjectives), sometimes you run into point-of-view problems. Point of view (often abbreviated "pov") refers to the vantage point from which a story is told. Entire books have been written about point of view, but for our purposes here, you will want to think about two things:

1. From what person is your story told?

First person: I went to the store.

Second person: You went to the store.

Third person: He went to the store.

2. From which character's point of view is your story told?

Many authors write novels in which some sections or chapters are told from one character's point of view and others are told from other characters' points of view. That's common and fine, but you do want to be sure that you don't switch point of view in the middle of a scene. Switching from one point of view to another in the midst of a section is often called a point-of-view slip (or, if it happens over and over, head-hopping). Point-of-view slips make it seem as though the author has no control over her writing, so you want to avoid them.

Point-of-view slips can sneak in easily through your dialogue tags if you are adding adverbs or adjectives to them. This is not a reason, on its own, to avoid adverbs and adjectives in tags—remember, sometimes they are very helpful—but it does mean you want to think carefully about them. Because those adverbs and adjectives are often functioning as shorthand for a longer, fuller description of the character who is speaking, sometimes they allow point-of-view slips that you would catch if you were writing a description of how the character looks or feels. Consider this exchange from Pete's point of view:

> *Pete inched closer to Kate on the couch. He ran a finger down her arm and tickled her lightly inside the elbow. "What do you say? Want to spend the night?"*

> *Kate flinched away from him. "Of course not," she said, disgusted.*

Because we're in Pete's point of view, we can be told anything about what Pete's doing, what he's thinking, how he's feeling, or what he can observe. We cannot know what he looks like in the moment (because he can't see himself) or what anyone else in the scene is thinking or feeling (because he does not have access to anyone else's thoughts or feelings). Everything in this scene is from Pete's point of view except for that last word, *"disgusted."* *"Disgusted"* is an adjective trailing along with the dialogue tag; it describes Kate's state of mind, but since Pete can't know that Kate is disgusted, this is a point-of-view slip. (Kate might be frightened rather than disgusted. She might have flinched because she hates being tickled and said *"Of course not"* because she wants to spend the night with Pete at *her* place.) Pete *could* observe behavior that suggests that Kate is disgusted, or he might speculate that she is disgusted. But as that line is presented, the reader is told, from Pete's point of view, that Kate is disgusted. Since he can't know whether she is or not, it's a point-of-view slip.

One way to remove that point-of-view slip would be to describe Kate's reaction more fully, thus suggesting her disgust without stating it outright:

Pete inched closer to Kate on the couch. He ran a finger down her arm and tickled her lightly inside the elbow. "What do you say? Want to spend the night?"

Kate flinched away from him and wrinkled her nose. "Of course not." She rubbed vigorously at the spot on her arm where he'd tickled her.

As when revising to avoid dialogue tags at all, adding more description removes the need for the adjective that caused the point-of-view slip. The description of Kate suggests disgust without stating it outright and without slipping out of Pete's point of view. You could also cast Kate's disgust as speculation from Pete:

Pete inched closer to Kate on the couch. He ran a finger down her arm and tickled her lightly inside the elbow. "What do you say? Want to spend the night?"

Kate flinched away from him. "Of course not," she said. The idea seemed to disgust her.

Here Kate's disgust remains an observation of Pete, so there's no slip out of his point of view.

Avoiding Unintentionally Suggesting Everything Happens at Once in Dialogue

Writers often tack phrases onto the end of dialogue tags to convey actions the characters are taking:

"Did you put your permission slip in your backpack?" Joey's mom asked as she wrapped his sandwich in wax paper.

or

"I love these things," I said, spinning faster and faster in my new swivel chair.

This is an excellent way to incorporate action into a scene and can allow you to vary sentence structure and make your writing livelier. However, sometimes those tacked-on phrases can suggest that two actions are occurring at the same time when logically they could not:

> *"Are you coming with us or not?" Shane asked, swallowing another sip of beer.*

The construction in the example above suggests that both actions in the sentence (*"asking"* and *"swallowing"*) happened simultaneously, but (unless he's very, very talented) Shane must have taken one of these actions before the other. Avoid these suggestions of improbable simultaneity by adding indications of the order in which the actions happened:

> *"Are you coming with us or not?" Shane asked before swallowing another sip of beer.*

or

> *"Are you coming with us or not?" Shane asked then swallowed another sip of beer.*

or

> *Shane swallowed another sip of beer then asked, "Are you coming with us or not?"*

KNOWING WHEN TO BREAK THE "RULES"

Following the suggestions I've laid out in this chapter will help you get your dialogue on the page in a way that keeps your prose lively and does not distract the reader. However, there will be times when you need to break some of these "rules." Confidence in knowing when to do so comes with experience, but here are some guidelines to help you decide if you have a situation that calls for breaking the rules:

1. Defaulting to said/asked as tags:

While it is generally a good idea to avoid sprinkling a dialogue exchange with different tags just for the sake of it, there will be times when you will want to vary your tags. Any time you wish to indicate specific ways of speaking (such as "whispering" or "shouting"), you should use whichever verb is appropriate in that instance. Long dialogue exchanges among three or more characters may also read better if you vary tags. In these instances, you may need to use tags often (since with more than two speakers in the scene, it may often be necessary to identify who spoke a particular line), and repeated use of "said" or "asked" may become annoying to readers.

Furthermore, "lied" is sometimes invaluable as a dialogue tag:

> *"Are you okay?" Donna asked.*

> *"I'm fine," David lied.*

While it would certainly be possible to explain that David is lying, doing so may not be necessary. If there's a strong reason based on plot or character to explain the lie, by all means do so. Something like this would certainly add to the reader's understanding of the scene and the character:

> *"Are you okay?" Donna asked.*

> *"I'm fine," David said. He didn't like lying to her, but now was not the time to get into all that was not fine with him.*

If you're thinking of using "lied" as a tag, consider point of view carefully. In the first example above, if the scene were in Donna's point of view, *"David lied"* would be a point-of-view slip. Donna might suspect David of lying, but she would have to speculate about it; the narrative could not say so as if it were a known fact:

> *"Are you okay?" Donna asked.*

> *"I'm fine," David said. But she knew he was lying.*

2. Asking tags to do too much:

While you want to be aware of when adverbs and adjectives in dialogue tags are standing in for description, you don't necessarily want to replace *all* of those adverbs and adjectives in tags with descriptions. Sometimes the best thing to do with an adverb or adjective in a tag is to delete it and replace it with nothing. Sometimes the scene just doesn't need any description of what a character is doing or saying (even the little that comes from an adverb or adjective) at a particular line. Very occasionally, the adverb or adjective in the tag is a good idea. Use your best judgment about any adverb or adjectives in tags you think are really needed. Just remember to ask yourself whether it will add something to the reader's understanding of scene or character, whether it should really be replaced with full description, whether it's a point-of-view slip, and whether you've already got tags with adverbs or adjectives at another point in the scene. If you answer yes, no, no, no to those questions, you might get away with that adverb or adjective you're considering in that dialogue tag.

3. Point-of-view slips:

Point of view can be very slippery, and sometimes two different people will disagree about whether something constitutes a slip. Consider, for example, this exchange (in Brian's point of view):

> *"I've never left the city. Ever. My entire life I've never been more than five miles from where we're standing right now," Brian said.*

> *"What!" Sarah said, flabbergasted. "Not ever?"*

Is that *"flabbergasted"* a point-of-view slip? Could Brian reasonably know, from what Sarah's said, from the way she's reacting, that she is, indeed, flabbergasted? In other words, is the state of being flabbergasted apparent enough that the reader will not question that Brian could observe it without having access to Sarah's thoughts or feelings? Different readers and writers will answer that question differently, with some calling it a point-of-view slip and others saying it's not. In situations like this one, you can usually get away with the point-of-view slip. Still, you want to avoid allowing too many of these "pseudo-slips" into your writing, because many scenes will likely work better with full description instead and also because the cumulative effect of several "pseudo-slips" might give the appearance that you don't have control over your point of view.

2:
MAKING DIALOGUE A SEAMLESS PART OF THE NARRATIVE

KEEPING THE SCENE GOING DURING DIALOGUE EXCHANGES

Sometimes your story can devolve into nothing *but* dialogue, especially during long exchanges. This effect is sometimes referred to as "talking heads" because without any gesture or action to anchor the dialogue exchange within the story, it can feel to a reader as if the characters have become nothing but heads floating in space while they speak to one another. Avoid the devolution of a scene into "talking heads" by making sure your characters continue to be fully realized during dialogue and that any action important to the scene continues to occur. Allow your characters to think, feel, act, and gesture throughout dialogue exchanges.

Here is an example of a dialogue exchange that devolves into "talking heads":

Alice set the tea tray on the coffee table and settled onto the couch. "Milk or lemon?" she asked.

"Oh, milk, of course," Lukas said.

Alice poured him a cup and passed it to him. She dropped a lemon slice into her own cup with an almost defiant plop. "I don't suppose there's any point in saying that all this clandestine stuff about having to come over right away and not being able to tell why on the telephone is utter nonsense."

"I don't suppose so, no."

"You can be such a pain, Lukas. I honestly don't know why Geoff puts up with you."

"I often wonder that myself."

"So what is it then?"

"What is what?"

"The reason you had to come over right away and couldn't say why on the telephone."

Notice how after the initial setup of the scene (setting down the tea tray and pouring the tea), everything but the dialogue falls away. The couch disappears, the coffee table and tea tray disappear, Alice and Lukas no longer (as far as the reader can see) have their teacups, and neither of them makes any gestures, feels anything, shifts in their seats, looks around the room, or anything. They do nothing but talk. The effect here is that the scene itself falls away, that the story seems to stop while the characters talk. You want to avoid this kind of cessation of scene because it creates dull, lifeless narrative instead of fully realized, engaging scenes. Allow the scene to be more than just a home for the dialogue; add gestures, actions, and interiority (access to the point-of-view character's thoughts and feelings) to any scene that turns into "talking heads" to keep the characters interesting, to let the reader know who those characters are and how they react to what's being said, and to keep the reader anchored in the setting of your story:

Alice set the tea tray on the coffee table and settled onto the couch. "Milk or lemon?" she asked.

"Oh, milk, of course," Lukas said.

Alice poured him a cup and passed it to him. She dropped a lemon slice into her own cup with an almost defiant plop. "I don't suppose there's any point in saying that all this clandestine stuff about having to come over right away and not being able to tell why on the telephone is utter nonsense."

Lukas stirred his tea slowly, the spoon making little clink clink sounds as it hit the sides of the delicate china cup. "I don't suppose so, no."

"You can be such a pain, Lukas." Alice blew on her tea, then took a noisy sip calculated to irritate her visitor. "I honestly don't know why Geoff puts up with you."

Lukas rested his teacup precariously on his knee and stared out the window with a faraway look on his face. "I often wonder that myself," he said softly.

Alice watched him for a moment, then put her cup down on the tray with a clatter. "So what is it then?"

Lukas startled, and some of his tea sloshed out of his cup and onto his trouser leg. "What is what?"

"The reason you had to come over right away and couldn't say why on the telephone."

In the above revision of the "talking heads" scene, both Alice and Lukas continue to act, continue to be *characters*, while they talk, and the reader learns about their attitudes toward each other and toward the conversation they're having rather than learning only what they say to one another. It certainly isn't necessary to accompany every line of dialogue in every scene with an action or gesture (that could become exhausting and begin to read as overdone), but include enough gesture, action, even description of characters or setting that are not tied to specific lines of dialogue (provided they are important to the scene) to keep the scene—not just the dialogue—alive.

HOW TO USE GESTURE EFFECTIVELY IN DIALOGUE

As you fill in your long dialogue exchanges with gesture and action to make them lively, engaging, fully developed scenes, be careful to avoid overusing generic gestures. Generic gestures are gestures that most people do but tell readers little to nothing about your characters. Some generic gestures include nodding, shaking the head, laughing, frowning, smiling, shrugging, snorting, rolling eyes, and raising eyebrows. If your dialogue exchange is full of gesture, but every one of those gestures is one of these generic sorts, your scene may be just as dull as if there were no gesture at all. And it will likely be repetitious as well. Perhaps worst of all, your reader may not know how to interpret the scene. With only the kinds of generic gestures that anyone might make in almost any situation, readers may not know whether characters are meant to be annoyed or sarcastic, pleased or cynical. A scene that is meant to be absurd and funny might come off as simply ridiculous and incoherent without characterizing gesture. Consider this short scene with no gesture:

Harry approached a friendly-looking stranger on the street corner. "Excuse me. Do you think you could help me?" he asked.

"I can give it a go," Sullivan said.

"Right. You see, I need to get to Curzon Street, but there seems to be a hole in my map. Do you know the way?"

"Can't help you there, I'm afraid. I avoid Curzon Street like the plague."

"Oh, really? Any particular reason?"

"I just can't stand the way it's spelled."

"I'm sorry. You did say the way it's spelled?"

"Yes."

"That's a bit peculiar, don't you think?"

"I quite agree. Perhaps you'd like to go to Park Lane instead."

The scene has certainly devolved into talking heads; there are no gestures or actions of any kind. Who are these men? What are they doing and feeling during this exchange? Are they having a laugh, or are they completely serious? Adding gesture and action should help answer those questions, but see how little generic gestures do to clear things up:

Harry approached a friendly-looking stranger on the street corner. "Excuse me. Do you think you could help me?" he asked.

"I can give it a go," Sullivan said.

"Right. You see, I need to get to Curzon Street, but there seems to be a hole in my map. Do you know the way?"

Sullivan shook his head. "Can't help you there, I'm afraid. I avoid Curzon Street like the plague."

"Oh, really? Any particular reason?"

Sullivan sniffed. "I just can't stand the way it's spelled."

"I'm sorry. You did say the way it's spelled?" Harry raised an eyebrow.

"Yes."

"That's a bit peculiar, don't you think?"

"I quite agree. Perhaps you'd like to go to Park Lane instead."

The added generic gestures (a shaken head, a sniff, a raised eyebrow) don't add much to the scene. The head shaking really only confirms something that is already clear in the dialogue (Sullivan's answer in the negative regarding whether he can help). The sniff suggests disgust or disdain, perhaps, but it doesn't tell the reader much that Sullivan's dialogue doesn't. The raised eyebrow does suggest something about Harry's reaction to Sullivan's explanation, but with so little else to characterize either Harry or Sullivan in the scene, it's still difficult to glean anything from the gesture. But specific gestures and actions—gestures and actions that are unique to Sullivan and Harry (or to the situation they find themselves in)—might tell the reader a lot (as well as make the scene itself more interesting).

Harry approached a friendly-looking stranger on the street corner. "Excuse me. Do you think you could help me?" he asked.

"I can give it a go," Sullivan said. He smoothed his tie and straightened his shoulders in an almost imperceptible maneuver.

"Right. You see, I need to get to Curzon Street, but there seems to be a hole in my map." Harry shook out his map, revealing that a circular chunk about the size of a biscuit was missing from it. "Do you know the way?"

Sullivan pursed his lips for a moment and then tsked. "I can't help you there, I'm afraid. I avoid Curzon Street like the plague."

"Oh, really? Any particular reason?" Harry tried to get the map to fold back into the size and shape it had been when he'd bought it.

"I just can't stand the way it's spelled."

Harry looked up from his efforts and raised his eyebrow. "I'm sorry. You did say the way it's spelled?"

Sullivan examined his shirt cuffs for a moment before saying, "Yes. "

"That's a bit peculiar, don't you think?"

Sullivan laid a hand on Harry's shoulder. "I quite agree. Perhaps you'd like to go to Park Lane instead."

If you're thinking that going from a scene with generic gestures to one with unique gestures looks an awful lot like going from a scene with talking heads to one with actions and gestures, you're right! Generic gestures *alone* do very little to enliven a scene. Any generic gesture might be helpful when used along with other unique and specific gestures (notice that Harry still raises his eyebrow in the revised scene above), but reliance on them alone will not result in an engaging scene that continues to move the narrative forward as the dialogue exchange unfolds. A scene using only generic gestures is hardly better than a scene with no gestures or actions at all.

Aside from being dull and not telling the reader much about what's going on with the characters in your scene, generic gestures can become very repetitious. The simplest way to avoid writing repetitious gestures is to be sure you use gestures specific to your characters. But since people do nod, shrug, smile, and so on, your characters may sometimes do so as well. So be on the lookout for scenes that become repetitious. Avoid scenes like this:

Jenna frowned. "But I don't like almonds."

Leo sighed. "I'm sorry, honey. That's all there is."

"I only like pecans."

"They don't have any pecans today. It's almonds or nothing."

Jenna sighed dramatically. "It's not fair."

Leo frowned. He hated disappointing her. "Let's see if they have some coconut chews instead."

Not only are Leo and Jenna engaging in nothing but generic actions in this exchange, but they're also engaging in the same two generic actions throughout. It's perfectly plausible that two people in a scene such as this might frown and sigh their way through it, but that doesn't make for an interesting dialogue exchange on the page. Giving them some other gestures that suggest the same moods and/or reactions as those sighs and frowns will keep the exchange from becoming repetitious:

Jenna wrinkled her nose. "But I don't like almonds."

Leo counted to ten slowly then leaned down to kiss his daughter on the top of the head. "I'm sorry, honey. That's all there is."

"I only like pecans."

"They don't have any pecans today. It's almonds or nothing."

Jenna sighed dramatically, pushing her bottom lip out almost comically. "That's not fair."

Leo frowned. He hated disappointing her. "Let's see if they have some coconut chews instead."

The rewritten scene avoids repeating any gestures. One of the original generic gestures (Jenna's frown) is replaced with a more specific description of what she does with her face. Leo's sigh is similarly shown to the reader instead of only identified and is made even more specific and unique to him by the addition of another gesture (the kiss on the head). The final two generic gestures from the original scene remain, though Jenna's sigh is made specific through additional description. Since the rest of the generic gestures have been edited out, there's no compelling need to remove Leo's last frown. People do frown, and with the presence of other specific, characterizing gestures in the scene and the absence of repeated generic gestures, Leo's frown is just fine.

AVOIDING LONG SEPARATIONS BETWEEN EXCHANGES

If you're writing dialogue exchanges that use gestures and action to keep the narrative alive during the exchange, you're going to be writing exchanges that contain a lot of stuff other than dialogue in them. That's great! As we've seen, dialogue exchanges that contain nothing but dialogue can become dull, boring, repetitive, and even confusing. But it's important to control how that other stuff gets on the page during dialogue. A dialogue exchange must remain an *exchange*, a back-and-forth between characters. If too much stuff gets in between two lines of dialogue, the sense of exchange can get interrupted, and the reader may lose track of what was happening in the dialogue. Consider this scene, in which one character engages in a long reverie before returning to the dialogue exchange:

> *Melody paused on her way down the hallway and leaned into Allie's office. "A bunch of us are going to go grab some lunch before the meeting. Want to come along?"*
>
> *Allie twirled her pen in her fingers. "Where you going?"*
>
> *"The Banshee. Liz says she can't go another day without fish and chips." Melody rolled her eyes.*
>
> *Allie stopped halfway out of her chair when Melody mentioned Liz. She and Liz had been avoiding each other for weeks, ducking around corners and slipping back into conference rooms whenever one of them caught sight of the other. Things had become nearly farcical between them. Allie had even hidden in a bathroom stall for a full five minutes the other day when she recognized the sound of Liz's high heels coming click-clicking into the room. She'd planned to slip out when Liz went into a stall, but*

then Liz had stood at the bathroom sink touching up her makeup and worrying at her hair. Allie had watched her through the crack between the stall door and the wall, chanting silently for Liz to leave so Allie could stop skulking like a child. Each of them blamed the other for the botched presentation that had cost the firm the Stewarts account, but they were both shying away from the blowup Allie knew in her bones was coming.

"I don't think I'd better," she said as she eased herself back into her chair.

A long separation like the one here between two lines of dialogue might be confusing to the reader. Some readers might hold Melody's last line in mind throughout the exposition about what's going on between Allie and Liz and be able to jump right back into the exchange with Allie's line. But some readers might forget what had been said over the course of that exposition. While it is easy enough for the reader to skim back to Melody's line and see what Allie is responding to, it's better if he doesn't have to. Avoid creating such a large separation between two lines of dialogue by moving part of any intervening long expositional section to another point in the scene:

Melody paused on her way down the hallway and leaned into Allie's office. "A bunch of us are going to go grab some lunch before the meeting. Want to come along?"

Allie twirled her pen in her fingers. "Where you going?"

"The Banshee. Liz says she can't go another day without fish and chips." Melody rolled her eyes.

Allie stopped halfway out of her chair when Melody mentioned Liz. She and Liz had been avoiding each other for weeks. Each of them blamed the other for a botched presentation that had cost the firm the Stewarts account, but they were both shying away from the blowup Allie knew in her bones was coming. She smiled at Melody and eased back into her chair. "I don't think I'd better."

After all the ducking around corners and slipping back into conference rooms whenever one of them caught sight of the other they'd done lately, Allie didn't think lunch was the time to try to sort things out. Things had become nearly farcical between them. Allie had even hidden in a bathroom stall for a full five minutes the other day when she recognized the sound of Liz's high heels coming click-clicking into the restroom. She'd planned to slip out when Liz went into a stall, but then Liz had stood at the bathroom sink touching up her makeup and worrying at her hair. Allie had watched her through the crack between the stall door and the wall, chanting silently for Liz to leave so Allie could stop skulking like a child.

Presenting the reader with just some of the information about why Allie doesn't want to see Liz before her last line of dialogue helps the reader understand where she's coming from and sets the reader up for the full explanation later, without asking her to hold half of a dialogue exchange in mind through a lengthy interruption of the exchange.

DIFFERENTIATING BETWEEN DIALOGUE AND DIRECT THOUGHTS

Especially if you are writing stories told in a close third-person point of view (a point of view using "he" or "she" that sticks very close to one character's experiences and feelings), confusion may arise over how to indicate characters' direct thoughts. A good rule of thumb is to treat any thoughts that could just as easily be dialogue as direct thoughts. Direct thoughts should be represented with italics. Consider the example below:

Jill wondered how much farther it was to San Francisco. *I bet I don't get there before dark*, she thought.

Jill's thought, *"I bet I don't get there before dark,"* behaves like dialogue. Jill could say exactly this out loud; therefore the thought is a direct thought and is set in italics. Note that what Jill wondered ("how much farther it was to San Francisco") is not in italics. Thoughts presented in this way are not *direct* thoughts, they do not behave like dialogue, and they are not set in italics.

Summary Dialogue

Summary dialogue is a neat little trick that lets you tell your reader the essence of what a character said without actually using dialogue. Summary dialogue gets its name because it summarizes what a character said rather than relaying exactly what was said. It can be useful when reporting actual dialogue might get in your way (if, for instance, you have a long descriptive passage during which one character says just one thing), when you simply want to put some variety into your presentation of dialogue, and in instances in which dialogue should be avoided (we'll take a closer look at times when dialogue should be avoided in Chapter Three). The following passage contains an example of summary dialogue:

> *That night they had a fight. Emily had gotten home from work late again and Akiro had forgotten to pick up milk from the store. They argued briefly and bitingly in the kitchen and then sat, arms folded, on either end of the couch, each staring ahead at the blank television screen. Their tabby cat launched herself through the room, executed a nifty end-over-end somersault, and settled down to wash. Emily smiled, and when Akiro looked her way, she didn't bother to hide it. He said something about what a blessing the cat had been, and she agreed, though through tight lips. Then, a few minutes later, she said she guessed he was a blessing—most of the time. They ended the night cuddling in front of an old black-and-white movie.*

The last three lines in this scene summarize three different lines of dialogue—Akiro's statement that the cat is a blessing, Emily's agreement, and her subsequent confession about him. This information could be presented as reported dialogue (a character's exact words appearing within quotation marks) on the page, but using summary dialogue allows you to incorporate their exchange into the description of the rest of the scene, which might be useful if you wished to emphasize an aspect of the scene other than the dialogue. If the essence of what your characters have said is more important than their actual words, consider summarizing their dialogue.

3:
BALANCING REALISM AND
NARRATIVE STYLE IN DIALOGUE

WHEN TO AVOID DIALOGUE

While most writers would agree that good writing incorporates some element of realism or believability (e.g., readers can believe that these specific characters would behave in these particular ways in this unique situation), it is important to remember that fiction should reflect the real world without necessarily being shackled to reporting something exactly as it would have happened in lived experience. You want to create realistic-sounding dialogue without it becoming so realistic that it's dull. (Much of what people say in daily speech is repetitive and uninteresting.) To this end, you want to develop a sense of when dialogue should be avoided. Sometimes characters need to say things to keep a scene moving along, but readers don't necessarily need to know *exactly* what they said.

A good test for whether you should report a character's dialogue exactly is to ask yourself what function the line of dialogue would serve. Any line of dialogue will always have at least one function, which is to tell the reader exactly what a character said. But a good line of dialogue will have at least one other function as well. Most commonly, a good line of dialogue's second function will have something to do with either the relation of important information or with characterization—that is, the line will show the reader something about how a character is feeling or thinking or what a character's temperament is. If a line of dialogue does not serve a second function, you may want to consider summarizing that dialogue rather than reporting it exactly. I discussed summary dialogue briefly in Chapter Two. Summary dialogue is an excellent tool for adding variety to your dialogue, but it is even more important to master the use of summary dialogue in those situations in which reported dialogue should definitely be avoided.

Avoid reported dialogue whenever a character's exact words are not important. Commonplace exchanges (exchanges that are likely to run basically the same way no matter who has them) may be the best example of times when readers do not need to know a character's exact words. Commonplace exchanges would include uninteresting greetings and partings (especially on the phone) and small talk that serves no other function in your story than that it is small talk. Consider this dialogue exchange:

My phone rang. "Hello?"

"Hello. Is that Rachel?"

"Yes."

"Hi, Rachel, it's Brad."

"Oh, hey, Brad."

"I was wondering if you might be able to watch Josie for me on Saturday."

This exchange is dull; until the last line, it doesn't tell the reader anything but that Brad has called Rachel, and it takes six lines of dialogue to do so. None of the dialogue has any purpose other than to report exactly what was said. Since what is really important here is that Brad called, summary dialogue can be used to get through that point quickly and on to the rest of this phone conversation, where presumably the interesting, characterizing, and plot-forwarding dialogue will happen. Summarizing this commonplace exchange might look something like this:

> *Brad called. "I was wondering if you might be able to watch Josie for me on Saturday," he said.*

This revision loses nothing of the content of the original. A reader would still know everything she knew from the first exchange, but the revised version cuts out dull, extraneous, single-function dialogue and gets right to the part that is important. Revise any commonplace greetings and partings in this way to cut right to the important dialogue, to the dialogue that has more than one function. (Remember, of course, that dialogue isn't necessarily dull and single function just because it takes place during a scene that *could be* commonplace. If, for instance, Rachel in the scene above knew it was Brad calling and answered the phone by saying, "Good afternoon, Rachel's Pretty Good Panty Emporium. How can I help you?" that would be dialogue worth reporting.)

As stated above, information exchange is one thing that can fulfill the "second function" test for reporting a character's exact words in dialogue, but you still want to be careful to avoid presenting exposition in dialogue. Unless it is important that readers hear an element of backstory or a plan or any other long piece of exposition in a particular character's own words (and sometimes it is!), present that exposition in narration rather than in dialogue. When the specific way or the exact words of such an explanation aren't important, simply indicate that the information was given by one character and then summarize the information itself:

> *Abby made herself comfortable on one of the couches and told us all about the tunnel under her grandfather's house. It originated in the cellar. Her uncles had starting digging through the back wall one summer when they were kids just for something to do. When their father caught them, he tanned their bottoms for them then declared the cellar off limits. It wasn't until years later that they discovered he'd expanded their tunnel, widening it and lengthening it and adding a door cleverly covered with sod and dirt to make it look like just another part of the earthen wall.*

This kind of summarizing is particularly useful when the reader has already seen an event taking place and it would be tedious to explain it all over again through dialogue. In the following scene, if the narrator's adventure in the gym had already been told, replaying the whole thing in dialogue would be dull. A quick summary to indicate that he told his friends about it and to highlight the key points is all that is necessary:

> *When I got back to the cafeteria, Tyrone and Erica would hardly let me eat for all their pestering me to tell them what had happened in the gym. So I told them in between bites of Meatless Casserole Surprise. I told them how I'd snuck into Coach Smith's office, about how I'd thought I'd been caught when Coach Johnson stepped halfway into the room and then changed her mind and went back out again, about rifling through Coach's filing cabinet until I found the fake rubber rat.*

WHAT TO AVOID IN DIALOGUE

Just as it is important to know when to avoid dialogue altogether, you also want to develop a sense of what kinds of things you should leave out of dialogue. Some aspects of real speech can be quite boring on the page, and your dialogue will be much more interesting and effective if you leave those kinds of things out. And some things simply don't work well on the page. The most common things you should avoid in dialogue are overuse of direct address, overuse of interjections and exclamations, clichés, and all capital letters.

Direct address refers to one character calling another character by name when speaking to that character. This example employs direct address:

> *"Thanks for all your help, Roger," George said.*

George is speaking to Roger and using his name to address him. (Note that when using direct address, the name is preceded by a comma if it comes after part of the dialogue—as in the example above—and is followed by a comma if it begins the line of dialogue: "Roger, thanks for all your help.") Direct address is perfectly fine if used occasionally. It can provide emphasis, lend intimacy to certain scenes, and help identify to whom dialogue is being addressed in exchanges with many characters. But overuse of direct address becomes annoyingly repetitive very quickly and often strikes readers' ears as *inauthentic* since most people do not address those they are speaking to directly very often. (Listen to a conversation happening around you. Once people get the attention of the person they want to talk to—"Hey, hon?" or "Jack, I need to talk to you"—they rarely use the person's name again unless for emphasis or to differentiate between speech meant for that person and that meant for another person in the vicinity.) Note the repetitiveness in this scene:

> *"Thanks for all your help, Roger," George said.*
>
> *"No problem, George. I'm always happy to lend a hand."*
>
> *"We appreciate it, Roger. Really."*
>
> *"Let me know if these colors don't work for you, George. I can probably scare up some more samples. Maybe in some different fabrics."*
>
> *"Will do, Roger."*

Almost infuriating, right? As long as it's clear to whom one character is talking, avoid direct address unless you have a strong reason to use it, such as emphasis or creating a sense of intimacy between two characters.

Similarly, avoid overusing interjections or exclamations in dialogue. Interjections are words that exclaim, protest, or command, and they often appear at the beginnings of sentences. Some common interjections include *wow*, *oh*, *well*, *no*, *ah*, *hey*, and *really*. Interjections usually have no grammatical function in a sentence, and while they can sometimes make dialogue sound more realistic, overusing them can seem like filler or lazy writing. Overuse of one particular interjection will also become repetitious. The following scene overuses interjections:

> *Joni hugged her old college roommate, then pulled back to study*

her face. "Oh, Tyra, it's so good to see you! I can't believe it's been four years since we've gotten together."

"No, it can't have been that long."

Joni steered Tyra toward a table at the back of the café. Once they were seated, she leaned forward and patted Tyra on the arm. "So, tell me all about everything. What have you been up to since graduation?"

"Well, I hung around New York for a year or so, just taking it all in, sharing an apartment with, like, four other girls. Then I decided to give the whole graduate school thing a try."

This relatively short exchange contains four interjections. Any one of them (with the possible exception of the "Oh, Tyra," which might read a little over the top in any case) would be fine if it didn't appear along with so many others so nearby. While real people may use interjections fairly frequently in real conversations, in the course of conversation, we tend to ignore them or accept them for what they are—placeholders, ways for us to gather our thoughts before speaking, or little indications of feeling. Readers, however, expect fiction to represent a realistic but streamlined version of the real world. We do not want to wade through placeholders in fiction unless those placeholders add something essential to our understanding of a character or a situation. Including one of those interjections from the scene above might lend a sense of realism to the dialogue exchange, and if chosen carefully, the interjection and its placement will tell the reader something about the character speaking (it will, like all good dialogue, serve a second function). See how much more cleanly the scene reads with most of the interjections edited out:

Joni hugged her old college roommate, then pulled back to study her face. "Tyra, it's so good to see you! I can't believe it's been four years since we've gotten together."

"It can't have been that long."

> *Joni steered Tyra toward a table at the back of the café. Once they were seated, she leaned forward and patted Tyra on the arm. "So, tell me all about everything. What have you been up to since graduation?"*

> *"I hung around New York for a year or so, just taking it all in, sharing an apartment with, like, four other girls. Then I decided to give the whole graduate school thing a try."*

If you're afraid that losing your interjections makes the dialogue too stark, try adding gestures or action that do the same kind of work as the interjection did. For example, a "well" often indicates hesitation or reluctance; in such a case, give your character something to do that suggests that same hesitation without using the "well":

> *Joni hugged her old college roommate, then pulled back to study her face. "Tyra, it's so good to see you! I can't believe it's been four years since we've gotten together."*

> *"It can't have been that long."*

> *Joni steered Tyra toward a table at the back of the café. Once they were seated, she leaned forward and patted Tyra on the arm. "So, tell me all about everything. What have you been up to since graduation?"*

> *Tyra shifted in her seat, crossing then uncrossing her legs. "I hung around New York for a year or so, just taking it all in, sharing an apartment with, like, four other girls. Then I decided to give the whole graduate school thing a try."*

Another aspect of everyday speech you want to try to avoid in dialogue is the cliché. Clichés are expressions (often quite imagistic and colorful ones) that have been repeated so often that they've become commonplace and no longer contain the spark of figurative language they may once have possessed. Phrases like "It's raining cats and dogs" and "bite the bullet" and "bury the hatchet" are clichés. People do use clichés in everyday speech, but clichés are uninteresting now *because* they have been used so often. While writers often accept that they should avoid clichés in narration, sometimes they still use them in dialogue, reasoning that since people do use clichés in real-life conversations, using them in dialogue makes it more realistic. However, avoiding clichés in dialogue is another example of tipping the scales toward making fiction more interesting than reality, and writing vivid, original dialogue instead of peppering your dialogue with clichés will result in more effective, if slightly less realistic, dialogue. Clichés also can often sound insincere, which will work against you if you mean for your characters to be having a heartfelt conversation.

To edit clichés out of your dialogue, think about what the cliché means, then try to find a way to express that idea differently. You might also consider whether the cliché is telling the reader something that might be better shown. Consider this exchange:

> Maggie sat on the bed and folded her legs under her. "He's breaking up with me, Dot. I can tell by the way he looks at me. Or maybe it's the way he doesn't look at me."

> Dot backed out of her closet and shook a button-up shirt to try to rid it of wrinkles. "You can't be sure of that. Men get distracted by all sorts of silly things. You'll go out tonight, and all the old zing will be back, you'll see."

> Maggie shook her head, and her curls bounced around her shoulders. "I don't think so." She traced the pattern on Dot's bedspread. "It's like he's lost all interest. He doesn't even try to fool around anymore."

> Dot shrugged. "Plenty of other fish in the sea."

Dot's response that there are *"plenty of other fish in the sea"* is a cliché. You might get away with that particular cliché in this scene, especially if you meant Dot to be dismissive and uncaring. (Like many of the things we've looked at, clichés are a bigger problem when they are used repeatedly rather than when any one cliché is used in a single instance.) But it may be better to unpack what Dot's cliché means and let her speak with unique phrases:

Maggie sat on the bed and folded her legs under her. "He's breaking up with me, Dot. I can tell by the way he looks at me. Or maybe it's the way he doesn't look at me."

Dot backed out of her closet and shook a button-up shirt to try to rid it of wrinkles. "You can't be sure of that. Men get distracted by all sorts of silly things. You'll go out tonight, and all the old zing will be back, you'll see."

Maggie shook her head, and her curls bounced around her shoulders. "I don't think so." She traced the pattern on Dot's bedspread. "It's like he's lost all interest. He doesn't even try to fool around anymore."

Dot shrugged. "If he's lost interest, maybe it's time to consider going with someone else. I hear Bobby Walton can't take his eyes off you."

Replacing that cliché does change the tenor of the scene a bit, but it also allows for more specificity. And because Dot says something more specific, the reader learns more about the situation. Her dialogue opens the scene up, creating more places for it to go, while the cliché effectively closes the scene down.

Last, avoid using all capital letters to express intense emotion or shouting in dialogue. This is perhaps more of a convention than an issue of writing craft, but all capitals can be distracting on the page and can suggest that the writer lacks confidence in her writing and is relying on those capital letters to convey something that should have been expressed in the writing itself. For instance, if strong emotion is suggested by your punctuation and dialogue tags, there's no need to use all caps, too:

"NO! I WON'T GO WITH YOU!" Donny shouted.

In the above example, the exclamation points and the indication that Donny is shouting are sufficient. The capital letters are distracting overkill; simply remove them:

"No! I won't go with you!" Donny shouted.

When all caps are used to suggest volume in speech, punctuation and clues from the text (like dialogue tags) nearly always convey that loudness well enough on their own. If the capital letters are standing in for emotion that is not suggested in any other way, remove the all caps and add a more specific indication of the emotion involved:

"I CAN'T GO THROUGH THIS AGAIN," Tim said. "It's just too much."

Here, it seems that Tim is not shouting but rather is feeling something deeply. The capitals are telling the reader that, but the scene will be much more effective if that emotion is shown. Allow actions and gestures to show that emotion:

Tim covered his face with his hands and hunched his shoulders. "I can't go through this again," he said. "It's just too much."

REPRESENTING ACCENTS

Opinions differ regarding the representation of accents in dialogue. Some writers think strong representation of accents on the page lends color and realism to a story, while others feel that representing accents in dialogue is simply distracting. If you feel you need to represent an accent on the page in order to fully capture a character or a setting, do so with a light touch. The accent should serve the telling of your story and should never distract from it. Accents on the page can be visually distracting and can be off-putting if the reader thinks the accent is represented incorrectly. You also run the risk, if you overdo an accent, of confusing your readers to the point that they don't know what characters are actually saying. A little goes a long way with accents; strive to suggest the accent you are aiming for rather than trying to capture it exactly as it sounds.

To this end, use alternate spellings of words sparingly and avoid turning your dialogue into an "apostrophe jungle," where the page swarms with apostrophes standing in for dropped letters. Choose one or two aspects of the accent you want to represent and use only those aspects in your dialogue. Allow those to stand in for the effect of the accent in its entirety. This will better convey the accent to your readers than trying to show exactly what the accent sounds like. Compare the following versions of the same dialogue, the first trying to represent an accent exactly, the second just suggesting it:

> *"It doont make no dif'rence to 'er. She gonna do what she want no 'ow."*

> *"It don't make no difference to her. She gonna do what she want no how."*

The second version is perhaps less accurate, but it also employs standard spellings more of the time and avoids an abundance of apostrophes. The second passage relies on the speaker's nonstandard grammar and sentence structure to suggest the accent, and in doing so is more readable. The more you can suggest an accent in this way and the less you rely on alternate spellings, the better. There's also no reason why you shouldn't tell the reader in the narration what the speaker sounds like. Telling the reader something like "Jamie had been born and bred in the Bronx and he sounded it" will go a long way toward helping your reader "hear" the accent you mean to imply, especially if you combine it with the particular vocabulary and syntax that suggest this in his dialogue. You can be more specific yet: "Darla had an unfortunate habit of dropping aitches from where they belonged and adding them where they didn't." Telling the reader something like this does not obligate you actually to drop Darla's aitches in her dialogue (in fact, it frees you from doing so).

4:
WAYS TO IMPROVE YOUR DIALOGUE

As with any aspect of writing, the best way to improve your dialogue is to practice. This chapter will suggest some ways you can practice writing dialogue using the pointers outlined throughout this guide and offers several exercises (with discussions) that will let you try your hand at improving some passages that make dialogue "mistakes."

READ YOUR DIALOGUE OUT LOUD

Because dialogue is meant to capture what people sound like when they speak, it can be very helpful to read your dialogue out loud to yourself. This should help you hear where the dialogue "clangs," where it comes off sounding like something no one would ever say. Pay particular attention to where you stumble over words, as this might suggest that something about your word choice is off. Reading your dialogue aloud may help you catch things like unintentional rhymes or bits that come off singsongy that you may want to edit out because they create an effect you did not intend. Likewise, you may notice that certain phrases sound harsher or too mealymouthed when spoken aloud. These could be indications that you want to edit that portion of the dialogue.

STUDY THE DIALOGUE OF A WRITER YOU ADMIRE

One of the best ways to improve any kind of writing is to read excellent examples of writing in that genre. Whenever you come across dialogue that really seems to *work* when you're reading, make note of that passage to study later. And then really study it. Read it out loud to see how it comes off the tongue. Note where the dialogue tags are placed, see where the gestures appear in relation to the dialogue itself, identify what the writer has done to strike a balance between realism (how people really sound when they talk) and fiction (making the dialogue work well on the page). You should make note of any dialogue you come across that sets your teeth on edge, too, and figure out what keeps it from working, though as you become more and more practiced at writing dialogue yourself, the examples of good writing will be more helpful to you.

One useful exercise many writing teachers suggest is copying down the writing you most admire. Take one of those good passages of dialogue you've noted and copy it (either by hand or by typing—whichever you typically use when you are composing yourself). The process of recreating that dialogue, line by line, word by word, comma by comma, will help you see how the lines are fitted together much more clearly than even studying them very carefully can. You will find yourself getting inside the writing, in a manner of speaking, and will understand better why the lines are crafted one way rather than another. When you do this exercise, of course, you should be sure to label what you've copied as someone else's work so that you don't stumble across it months later and, forgetting that it is not your own, think what a wonderful bit of dialogue you've found that you ought to slot into your current project!

TUNE YOUR EAR

In addition to paying close attention to the dialogue in any fiction you read, tune into any conversations you hear around you. While you won't want to use any dialogue you overhear word for word (this would be fairly unethical, as well as running counter to some of the issues discussed in Chapter Three), listening carefully to the way real people speak will help you create dialogue that sounds realistic. You might also study any dialogue you particularly like in TV shows, movies, and plays in the same way you might study the dialogue in books you like. Do be aware, however, that some of the aspects of realism (such as oral crutches—"um," "like," "etcetera"—and interjections) that tend not to read well on the page can come off much better in TV or movies (because, just as in real conversations, we tend to pass over these things when we hear them rather than read them). Take note of how the dialogue works and consider how it would have to be altered if it were going to appear on the page instead of on screen.

EXERCISE PROMPTS

Below are four exercise prompts that will help you practice improving your dialogue. After you have done the exercises, see "Discussions of Exercise Prompts" for discussions of each exercise.

1. Turn an overheard conversation into dialogue

Record a conversation happening around you, and then transcribe that conversation exactly as it appears on the recording. Once you have the transcript, revise it into a dialogue exchange that would be appropriate for inclusion in fiction by adding actions and gestures and revising the dialogue itself. (Remember that this is just an exercise for your own private use. Actually using someone's exact words in your fiction without their knowledge would be unethical.)

2. Improve the dialogue in this passage:

Heather cornered Walter in the hallway near his locker. "I hear there's going to be a party on the beach Friday night," she said. "Want to go?" Walter shrugged.

He said, "I'm not really into the beach."

"What!" she blurted. "How can anyone live in Florida all their life and not be into the beach?"

"I'm just not," he told her as he pulled his chemistry book out from behind his gym bag. "Besides, I haven't lived here all my life. I'm from Ohio."

"Ohio? Boring. *All the more reason. Come on, come with us.*"

"Who's 'us'?"

"Just some of the crowd. You know, all the cool kids."

"Which *cool kids? The cool kids all hate me.*"

"No, they don't. They just don't know you yet."

"I dunno. Maybe."

3. Improve the dialogue in this passage:

Steam poured out from under the hood of Birdie's Toyota. Julia pulled the kerchief from around her hair and used it to cover her hand as she threw up the hood. "Overheating, all right."

"What do we do?" Birdie asked.

"Is there any water left in the thermos from lunch?"

"No! I drank the last of it when I took the pill for my headache. What are we going to do?"

"Do you have your cell phone?"

"I left it at home," Birdie said. "I know how you hate them. I just wanted to have a nice afternoon with no interruptions!"

"We start walking then, I guess. If your head can take it. There was a nice big tree back up the road just a piece. We could sit

there in the shade until you feel a little better. Or until someone comes along."

"Oh, Julia!"

4. Improve the dialogue in this passage:

Hector folded and refolded a sheet of his math homework until it took the triangular shape of a paper football. "Heads up," he said, just seconds before he took aim and flicked it toward Maria across the table.

The football hit Maria on the forehead then fell to the table in front of her. She stared at her textbook for a moment before slapping her hand over the football. "I have to study, Hector. Don't you?"

He shrugged. "Only one more test before the final exam. I figure I can mess this one up pretty good and still be all right if I do well on the final."

Maria sighed. "But why risk it?"

Hector shrugged. "I don't feel like studying today."

"Do you ever?"

"No. Sometimes Mama makes me, though." He grinned. "You should see her on a tear."

"I can imagine. I'd rather study. And you should, too." Maria flicked the paper football back to his side of the table and bent her head over her book once more.

Hector shrugged, then unfolded the football, smoothed it out, and tried to read the formulas written there in now-smudged pencil.

5. Improve the dialogue in this passage:

Dr. Greene dropped into his chair, flipped his clipboard onto his desk, and motioned toward the extra chair in the room. Dr. Friedman sat and carefully crossed her legs, giving her skirt a little tug so that the hem just brushed the top of her knee.

"Well, Violet, I just don't know what to tell you," Dr. Greene said. "Our policies are clearly laid out in the employee handbook."

Dr. Friedman shifted almost imperceptibly in her chair. "I was hoping you'd be able to offer me some advice, Luke. I'm at the end of my rope here."

"Well, I suppose we could invite Mr. Miller in for a sit-down, just us three, and talk it out. But I really think you ought to bite the bullet and report him, Violet, I really do."

Dr. Greene dropped her head into her hands. "I don't know, Luke. I just don't know." She looked up at him, and her face was splotchy and red, as if she'd somehow managed to have an entire crying jag in the few seconds her face had been hidden. She pounded her fist against the armrest on the chair. "I CAN'T TAKE THIS ANYMORE."

Dr. Friedman came around his desk, knelt down in front of her, and took her hand. "It's okay, Violet. We'll find a way to deal with him. I promise."

DISCUSSIONS OF EXERCISE PROMPTS

1. Turn an overheard conversation into dialogue

This exercise is designed to help you think about the balance you want to strike between fiction and reality in your writing. Unless you recorded some exceptionally erudite and eloquent conversationalists, your transcript is likely to be full of oral crutches, interjections, pauses, stumbled words, uninteresting and/or commonplace exchanges, and so on. Of course, this is how people really talk. But most of the time, this is not what makes for interesting reading. In your revision, you should have added dialogue tags as necessary (Chapter One, "Dialogue Tags"); added characterizing gestures (Chapter Two, "Keeping the Scene Going during Dialogue Exchanges" and "How to Use Gesture Effectively in Dialogue"); removed uninteresting, commonplace exchanges (Chapter Three, " When to Avoid Dialogue"); removed long pauses or filled them with interesting action (Chapter Two, "Keeping the Scene Going during Dialogue Exchanges"); removed interjections and stumbling over words except in one or (in the case of a long exchange) two choice instances where they are characterizing or otherwise very important (Chapter Three, "What to Avoid in Dialogue"); and carefully considered when and how to replace clichés with more original language (Chapter Three, "What to Avoid in Dialogue"). The general effect should be that your revised dialogue exchange contains largely the same content as the conversation you recorded but should be presented in a streamlined and more interesting (for the reader) fashion.

2. Below is one possible revision of this dialogue exchange. Your revision might be slightly different. The lines are lettered to aid in the discussion found below the revised passage.

A. *Heather cornered Walter in the hallway near his locker. "I hear there's going to be a party on the beach Friday night. Want to go?"*

B. *Walter shrugged. "I'm not really into the beach."*

C. *"What!" She widened her eyes comically and slapped his arm. "How can anyone live in Florida all their life and not be into the beach?"*

D. *"I'm just not," he said as he pulled his chemistry book out from behind his gym bag. "Besides, I haven't lived here all my life. I'm from Ohio."*

E. *"Ohio? Boring. All the more reason. Come on, come with us."*

F. *"Who's 'us'?"*

G. *"Just some of the crowd. You know, all the cool kids."*

H. *Walter narrowed his eyes. "Which cool kids? The cool kids all hate me."*

I. *"No, they don't. They just don't know you yet."*

J. *"I dunno. Maybe."*

Discussion: In line A, Heather's dialogue tag is unnecessary. It is clear that she is speaking because there is an action attached to her line. Line B moves Walter's action in response to Heather (his shrug) to its own line and removes Walter's tag, as it is also not necessary once his action is properly accompanying his line of dialogue. (Note that *were* Walter's dialogue tag necessary, you would probably want to move it to the end of the sentence: "I'm not really into the beach," he said.) Line C removes a dialogue tag that is unnecessary (because of her accompanying action) and that is a "bad" tag because it tries to do too much. The revision allows the punctuation and description to more fully evoke what the tag tried to do. Line D adds a needed comma between Walter's line of dialogue and the tag. "He told her" is also replaced with "said," since it should be clear without saying so explicitly that Walter must still be speaking to Heather. Line H adds an identifying gesture to help readers keep track of who says which line in the span from lines E through I. The issues appearing in this passage are discussed in Chapter One.

3. Below is one possible revision of this dialogue exchange. The action in this exchange falls away completely as the dialogue goes on. The action in this scene might play out in any number of ways, so it is unlikely that your revision will look much like the one below. But as long as you found a way to keep Birdie and Julia in the scene and kept the action going around them while they talked, you are on the right track. Review Chapter Two, "Keeping the Scene Going during Dialogue Exchanges", for the full discussion of keeping the action going during a dialogue exchange.

Steam poured out from under the hood of Birdie's Toyota. Julia pulled the kerchief from around her hair and used it to cover her hand as she threw up the hood. "Overheating, all right."

Birdie peered toward the engine block without actually moving any closer to it. "What do we do?" she asked.

Julia shook out her kerchief and tied it back around her hair. It was far too hot to stand it touching her shoulders for long. "Is there any water left in the thermos from lunch?"

Birdie's face lit up for a moment but then fell. "No! I drank the last of it when I took the pill for my headache." She touched her temple lightly, as if remembering the pill had also reminded her that her head did actually ache. "What are we going to do?"

"Do you have your cell phone?"

"I left it home. I know how you hate them." Birdie seemed about to cry. Her shoulders hunched for a moment under the

light sweater Julia couldn't imagine wearing in this heat. "I just wanted to have a nice afternoon with no interruptions!"

Julia pursed her lips. Of all the times for Birdie to have cared about Julia's stupid dislike of cell phones and left hers home. What did she mean by it? "We start walking then, I guess." She pushed past Birdie to collect their handbags from the backseat. But the sight of Birdie's tiny purse, which matched her sweater so perfectly, suddenly made her feel warm toward her friend. She shouldered her own bag and handed Birdie hers. She squeezed Birdie's shoulder. "If your head can take it. There was a nice big tree back up the road just a piece. We could sit there in the shade until you feel a little better. Or until someone comes along."

"Oh, Julia!"

4. Below is one possible revision of this dialogue exchange. Your revision might be slightly different. The lines are lettered to aid in the discussion found below the revised passage.

Hector folded and refolded a sheet of his math homework until it took the triangular shape of a paper football. "Heads up," he said, just seconds before he took aim and flicked it toward Maria across the table.

The football hit Maria on the forehead, then fell to the table in front of her. She stared at her textbook for a moment before slapping her hand over the football. "I have to study, Hector. Don't you?"

A. *"Only one more test before the final exam. I figure I can mess this one up pretty good and still be all right if I do well on the final."*

B. *Maria tapped her pencil against the table. "But why risk it?"*

C. *Hector shrugged. "I don't feel like studying today."*

"Do you ever?"

D. *"No. Sometimes Mama makes me, though." He grinned. "You should see her on a tear."*

"I can imagine. I'd rather study. And you should, too." Maria flicked the paper football back to his side of the table and bent her head over her book once more.

E. *Hector twirled the football in his fingers, then unfolded it, smoothed it out, and tried to read the formulas written there in now-smudged pencil.*

This passage successfully avoids turning into "talking heads," but many of the gestures filling out the scene are generic, and because some of them appear more than once in such a short passage, they become repetitive as well. Make the scene livelier by removing unnecessary generic gestures and replacing some generic gestures with more interesting, more characterizing action. In line A, the revision simply removes the generic gesture (a shrug). Remember that not every line of dialogue needs a gesture or action accompanying it. In line B, the generic gesture (a sigh) is replaced with a different gesture that tells the reader a little more about the character. Line C retains the generic gesture (a shrug). Generic gestures have their place; the problem arises when they are overused or never accompanied by any gestures or actions that are unique to the characters. This revision leaves the generic gesture in line D, since it is the only gesture denoting something like a smile in this passage, but you may have chosen to replace it. Line E replaces a generic (and, in the original, repeated) gesture (a shrug) with a more characterizing gesture. The issues appearing in this section are discussed in Chapter Two, "How to Use Gesture Effectively in Dialogue."

5. Below is one possible revision of this dialogue exchange. Your revision might be slightly different. The lines are lettered to aid in the discussion found below the revised passage.

Dr. Greene dropped into his chair, flipped his clipboard onto his desk, and motioned toward the extra chair in the room. Dr. Friedman sat and carefully crossed her legs, giving her skirt a little tug so that the hem just brushed the top of her knee.

A. *"I just don't know what to tell you," Dr. Greene said. "Our policies are clearly laid out in the employee handbook."*

B. *Dr. Friedman shifted almost imperceptibly in her chair. "I was hoping you'd be able to offer me some advice, Luke. I'm at the end of my rope here."*

C. *"Well, I suppose we could invite Mr. Miller in for a sit-down, just us three, and talk it out. I know it may be difficult for you, but I think you should report him, I really do."*

D. *Dr. Greene dropped her head into her hands. "I don't know. I just don't know." She looked up at him, and her face was splotchy and red, as if she'd somehow managed to have an entire crying jag in the few seconds her face had been hidden. She pounded her fist against the armrest on the chair. "I can't take this anymore."*

E. *Dr. Friedman came around his desk, knelt down in front of her, and took her hand. "It's okay, Violet. We'll find a way to deal with him. I promise."*

Line A removes an interjection ("well") and an instance of direct address, as overuse of both can make a scene read repetitious and inauthentic. Line B contains both an instance of direct address and a cliché, but both have been left in. One of the first instances of direct address in the passage should probably stay in to indicate that these doctors are on a first-name basis. Clichés do not need to be removed entirely from dialogue; the occasional cliché, especially one like this ("I'm at the end of my rope") that is something someone is very likely to say in the moment, can lend realism to a scene. Line C leaves in an interjection ("well," again), as the occasional interjection can lend realism to a scene, and this "well" seems the more important of the two in the passage. A second cliché ("bite the bullet") has been replaced with a plain-speech indication of the same idea. Another instance of direct address has been removed at line D, along with a sentence in all caps. Dr. Friedman's actions convey the emotion of her line of dialogue without resorting to all caps. Finally, the revision leaves in the final instance of direct address at line E, since this helps show Dr. Greene's feelings for Dr. Friedman. The issues appearing in this passage are discussed in Chapter Three.

ABOUT THE AUTHOR

Laura E. Koons completed graduate degrees in Creative Writing at both Ohio University and University of Tennessee. She has worked on several literary magazines including *Quarter After Eight* and *Grist: The Journal for Writers*, where she served as a fiction editor for the inaugural issue. She is currently a reader for *Drunken Boat: an online journal of art and literature*. Laura likes reading best of all, but she also spends considerable time volunteering at her local library and working on her own writing projects. She currently works for Red Adept Publishing and lives in Virginia with her husband and two snarky cats.

www.ingramcontent.com/pod-product-compliance
Lightning Source LLC
LaVergne TN
LVHW041219080426
835508LV00011B/999